DARKNESS ILLUMINATED

Platforms at the National Theatre

The National Theatre's *Platforms* have provided an eclectic programme of pre-performance events celebrating all aspects of the arts, offering the chance to learn about the National's work and discover more about theatre in general. Platforms are produced by Angus MacKechnie.

www.nationaltheatre.org.uk/platform

DARKNESS ILLUMINATED

PLATFORM DISCUSSIONS ON
'HIS DARK MATERIALS'
AT THE NATIONAL THEATRE

Philip Pullman
Nicholas Hytner
Dr Rowan Williams
Nicholas Wright
and others

in conversation with
ROBERT BUTLER

BLOOMSBURY ACADEMIC
Bloomsbury Publishing Plc
50 Bedford Square, London, WC1B 3DP, UK
1385 Broadway, New York, NY 10018, USA
29 Earlsfort Terrace, Dublin 2, Ireland

BLOOMSBURY, BLOOMSBURY ACADEMIC and the Diana logo
are trademarks of Bloomsbury Publishing Plc

First published by National Theatre and Oberon 2004
Reprinted by Bloomsbury Academic, 2024

A catalogue record for this book is available from the British Library.

A catalogue record for this book is available from the Library of Congress.

ISBN 978-1-840-02455-5 paperback

To find out more about our authors and books visit www.bloomsbury.com
and sign up for our newsletters.

CONTENTS

Robert Butler is the author of three books in the series 'The National Theatre at Work': *Humble Beginnings, Just About Anything Goes,* and *The Art of Darkness* (published with Oberon). From 1995–2000 he was drama critic of the *Independent on Sunday*.

Introduction

Robert Butler

It's one thing to interview an actor, director or playwright about a show before it opens. It's quite another to interview the same people once the public and critics have been in to judge for themselves. I had followed the rehearsals of *His Dark Materials* at the National Theatre from the early workshops and design meetings in summer 2003, through ten weeks of rehearsals in the autumn, to the technicals, previews and, finally, opening performances in the week before Christmas.

Along the way I had spoken to as many of the participants as I could about what was happening and why: from the author Philip Pullman and director Nicholas Hytner, to the cast in the rehearsal room and the production team in the workshops, as they assembled the sets, puppets, costumes and props.

In his study near Oxford, Philip Pullman had told me that the National Theatre had set itself a very difficult task. "I don't think anything is impossible in the theatre. But it is going to be terribly difficult."

In his office overlooking the Thames, Nicholas Hytner had told me: "I could be wrong about the whole thing. It might simply not work."

In the National Theatre restaurant, the adapter Nicholas Wright had acknowledged the concern of millions of Pullman fans. "Every departure from the book has been wrested from us, almost unwillingly, but it has always been to make it more of a play."

In the rehearsal room, Anna Maxwell Martin, who played Lyra, and Dominic Cooper who played Will, had explained how—as actors in their twenties—they were hoping to be convincing as twelve year olds. "We're not kids,"

Anna said, "All we can get is the energy of a kid. Thinking in the way a child thinks rather than how an adult thinks." Dominic agreed. "It's the things the characters do that reveal their age. We would never in a million years jump through a window into another universe."

How could a 1300-page novel possibly be turned into a six-hour play? I described how this vast enterprise took shape in a behind-the-scenes book *The Art of Darkness— Staging the Philip Pullman Trilogy*. I handed the text in the morning after the first performance of Part Two. A week later it was published.

Two weeks after that, *His Dark Materials* officially opened, and anyone who was interested could discover in the news sections and the arts pages of the national press whether the show had been a hit or whether—a possibility its director had always conceded—it had simply not worked.

Three days after the press night, I went back to the National to ask a few more questions. During the run of *His Dark Materials* there was to be a series of 'Platform' discussions about the production. This time the interviews would be on stage and in front of an audience.

Only a couple of weeks had passed, but the director, novelist, adapter, actors and production team—and an unusually distinguished member of the audience—were now able to offer a new perspective on what had taken place. For the first time, those who had staged *His Dark Materials* had a reliable idea of what it was they had created. The first batch of reviews for the play had already appeared. *The Evening Standard* called it an "astonishing epic of narrative and theatrical invention". The *Observer* said "Pullman's magical fantasy becomes a National treasure".

Each Platform discussion took place at 6pm on the Olivier stage, often in front of the tree and bench in the Botanic Garden, which form the opening and closing scene of the production. The discussions lasted 45 minutes: usually I asked questions for half an hour and members of the audience asked theirs for the final fifteen minutes. What follows is almost the entire transcript of each conversation.

The first interviewee, Nicholas Hytner, spoke of why adult actors had to play twelve-year-olds, what had happened to the Mulefas, what was the hardest thing of all about being a director, and how you know a production is working.

Philip Pullman told the audience what he thought of the production and how it differed from the books. He described what kind of twelve-year-old he had been and why that age—Will and Lyra's age—is such an important turning-point in a person's life. He was momentarily stumped when a member of the audience asked what happened when a daemon was born.

Nicholas Wright described how he had set about turning the books into plays and why certain characters had to go. He also spoke of what he had in common with Lyra (they both had absent fathers), how he had a childhood passion for puppetry and how his experience as a child actor paralleled one of the plays' main themes.

The production team gave an awesome sense of the scale of the staging, from listing the number of people working backstage to pinpointing the single person responsible for announcing a thousand cues each performance. The tree in the Botanic Garden (standing just behind them) provided an example of the many materials, departments and weeks involved in creating a single element of the production.

The Platform discussion that attracted the most publicity was the one between the Archbishop of Canterbury, Dr Rowan Williams, and Philip Pullman. The entire conversation was published in the *Daily Telegraph*. A few days before, Dr Williams had spoken at Downing Street about Religious Education in schools and had recommended *His Dark Materials*—the novels and the plays. That comment alone had put the production on the front page of the *Guardian*.

During the Platform, Dr Williams outlined the kind of context in which the books and the plays might be explored. Philip Pullman and Dr Williams discussed the absence of Jesus from the novels and plays and—in the light of Mel Gibson's new film *The Passion of the Christ*—Dr Williams nominated one of his favourite religious films.

In the final week of the run, Anna Maxwell Martin and Dominic Cooper explained what it had been like to act together for six months, what it was like to play twelve-year-olds, how their performances had changed during the run and how a scene that had never worked in rehearsals came alive in front of an audience.

If the first batch of interviews had been conducted when the participants were still inching their way forward in the dark, this second batch was conducted after they had experienced the full glare of public attention. It was a short but decisive step that took them from the views expressed in *The Art of Darkness* to those in *Darkness Illuminated*.

RB
July 2004

1

The Director

Nicholas Hytner
Olivier Theatre, 6 January 2004

Robert Butler: I want to take you right back to the first time you read the books. What made you think that you could stage them?

Nicholas Hytner: I think what really felt they belonged on stage were the central relationships: the young girl locked in this really heart-wrenching quest to find parents to love, *someone* to love; the tremendous ambiguity of her relationship with her mother, her father, discovering who they are; her meeting with a boy who is also searching for a parent, also searching for love. Essentially that simple story about two very young people discovering what love is and then losing it. Without that, I wouldn't have felt it was stageable. That central story is eminently stageable, and if it works, it works largely because the central actors keep that story alive and burn it into the audience's consciousness. Yes, it does look unstageable, but ultimately there's always a solution to creating a stage world. The daemons felt like a major challenge, certainly, something that would have to be solved using techniques I'd never explored before. There were all sorts of major and worrying challenges, technically, but the heart of the story felt as if it belonged on stage.

When you had your first meeting with Philip Pullman, was he surprised at your request?

When I first got in touch with Philip it was before *The Amber Spyglass* won the Whitbread Prize, and I think he was surprised at the extent to which the books had taken off (in the last two years they have taken off even more). I think our request was no more nor less surprising to him than anything else. He had been a very well-regarded children's author and was just getting used to being a national phenomenon.

Once you'd acquired the rights, was your first step to find an adapter?

Yes. The first step was to think about who could write the play. I'd worked with Nicholas Wright before. I knew him to be a wonderfully sympathetic adapter of other people's material, and somebody I get on with terribly well, we speak the same language. I asked him if he'd read the books and it turned out he'd read them long before I had, so it seemed the obvious thing.

You didn't look to someone who specialised in writing for young people?

No, because the books don't talk down to young people. It's been much remarked about Philip Pullman's work that he, essentially, writes for adults. Once kids are twelve, they don't want to be treated like kids any more.

There were three books. Did you think about just staging the first one?

No. We did think about one play, two plays or three. One play was obviously never going to be possible. Three plays we did think about quite a lot, and it just felt that was too much to ask of an audience, particularly a family audience: to come to the theatre three times, or if you are seeing them all in one day to come in the morning and stay all day. To ask four people to pay three times—that was never going to work. So early on we thought we should try to do it in two plays, which immediately presented the first narrative problem: negotiating our way through the end of *Northern Lights* into the first half of *The Subtle Knife* without making it seem as if Play One was ending three quarters of an hour too soon. That was a problem which hung around for quite some time. It took a while for the second half of Play One not to feel broken-backed.

After you'd recruited Nicholas Wright, who were the next people to come on board?

The design team was next. I'd worked separately with Giles Cadle, the set designer, and Jon Morrell, the costume designer. Then quite early on, in the autumn of 2002, the three of us went out to meet with Michael Curry, the puppet designer, at his workshops in Oregon. So we had that team very early on.

And then you had a workshop...

Yes, the first workshop was at the end of 2002. We had a certain amount of material from Play One, we had very little in the way of prototype puppetry. Several of the current company took part in that workshop. Sam Barnett, who plays Pantalaimon, is the only one who has done literally everything—every workshop, every reading, and the show. But the first workshop was very rudimentary. We did some improvising, we explored different ways of being bears... We kind of knew at that stage what the principle of the daemon puppetry would be, but during that workshop they were green socks, on hands.

What were the kinds of ideas you discarded at that point?

There were lots of terrible ideas. One was to have elaborate mimes every time the alethiometer was read, in fact the whole stage floor was going to be an alethiometer. There was lots of "out-front" story-telling, as there had been in *Nicholas Nickleby*. It was halfway through that workshop when we thought that technique, brilliant in its day, had *had* its day and that we should try to make a real play out of it all. Another idea was that, every time she read the alethiometer, this mysterious boy with a green leather folder wandered into the mime, and Lyra kept wondering what he had to do with her story. You have to go through these things to realise they are superfluous.

Did you still think at that stage that you might not go any further with the project?

Yes, that first workshop was very much "Will we still do this or not?" and though at its end we still didn't have anything like a script, we felt we had enough confidence in our ability to turn it into theatrical material to proceed. What happened after that was a three-day reading of what were then two plays, in the spring of last year. Then in the summer of last year we did a two-week workshop when we had further drafts of both plays, which we thought, before we went into the workshop, were pretty close to what we needed. That was a very miserable and depressing workshop because it transpired that the scripts were nowhere near ready. So what we ended up doing was thrashing through bits of it, then quite often sending the actors away while Nick Wright, Giles Cadle and I agonised over what we had to do to make something work that wasn't. It was miserable but extremely productive. After that two-week workshop, I think we just spent a single day reading the whole thing again, and it did then seem nearer to ready.

This was a project in which the designer played a very critical part in telling the story.

Yes, there came a point in the summer of last year, where once the basic architecture of the set was designed and seemed to be appropriate, it was sometimes necessary for the designer to say, "I need two pages more here to get us to the next bit". That never meant two superfluous pages being added; it always meant material from one scene would be worked into another scene, in order for something to happen within the drum revolve. Every time the drum goes down, time is needed to adapt what's within the drum so that next time it appears, it delivers what it needs to deliver. When what we call the portcullis, the big backdrop, comes down for stuff to be changed behind it, time is needed for that change to happen. For Nick Wright and me it was very like working on a screenplay. Very often when you're working on a film with a writer, you're called halfway through the location scout by someone saying, "We simply can't afford to go to two locations on the Friday in the third week, so that scene you've got in the carpark must now happen in the bathroom of the country house." That kind of writing is relatively straightforward to do.

It must be harder to know if an actor is going to be any good as an armoured bear or a Gallivespian.

Yes, it was about finding really good, warm-spirited actors, who were up for anything and to whom you felt you could throw any challenge. That's the company we got together. Obviously getting Will and Lyra right was central. But otherwise you're casting the way you generally cast—looking for people you've worked with before, or who've worked here before, and people who will connect with a part. A huge number of this company are simply marvellous, versatile and physically very inventive actors who I felt would work together well to create all these different worlds.

How early on was the decision taken to cast actors in their twenties, like Anna Maxwell Martin and Dominic Cooper, to play Lyra and Will?

Oh, immediately. It never occurred to me to cast twelve-year-old actors. There are so many reasons why not. It would simply be impossible for any twelve-year-old actor to carry a play in this theatre. I'd go further and say it's impossible for a twelve-year-old actor to carry a big play virtually anywhere, though a twelve-year-old actor can carry a movie. So much of a twelve-year-old actor's performance in a movie can be created in the cutting room. It's a matter of stamina, vocal resource, concentration and imagination. Let's take concentration first. There isn't a twelve-year-old who can stay there for six hours and hold it together. It's hard for an adult. Then vocal stamina: you really don't want to listen to a twelve-year-old's untrained voice for six hours. It's through the voice, through Anna and Dominic's trained voices and trained sensibilities that the wide range of emotions of those two characters is conveyed. I think it's a straightforward and conventional acting challenge for a 25-year-old actor to come on stage and say, "I'm twelve." If the actor is convincing enough, you believe the actor's twelve. But for a twelve-year-old actor to come onto the stage and say, "Believe every single thing I'm going through", is much harder. The hard things are the emotional twists and turns, having the energy and the imagination and the expertise not just to perform the moment but to take you through the scene and then to carry that scene into the next. These things take training and experience. So it was never going to be a twelve-year-old. The next question was inevitably, Could it possibly be an actress in her early twenties? This stage, the Olivier, is basically the hardest to work in the country. It was, consciously or not, conceived for the kind of actor whose name the theatre bears, to stand centre-stage and deliver in the old, heroic style. It's been a challenge ever since the theatre was built to find the actors who can effortlessly carry this theatre, even in the classics, the great public plays of the Elizabethan and Jacobean eras. It was kind of miraculous to find an actress in her early twenties to carry two plays.

Early on you said to the cast, "No child acting". What did you mean by that?

I think the danger when adults play children is that they can be fantastically patronising in the way they show you what children are like. I hear it on radio all the time. I decided we should never do that, never ape children's mannerisms. I think and hope that all the actors who play twelve-year-olds in the show succeed in not being patronising to twelve-year-olds.

It seemed to me that you had to take rather more decisions before rehearsals started than perhaps you would have had to on another production.

Practical decisions had to be taken, again almost like making a movie, because, scene by scene we had to know where the set was moving. It's much easier to be fluid if you're starting with more or less nothing. With the last show I did here, *Henry V*, we were able to be fluid because we were using an empty stage, a wall, and a couple of very cheap Jeeps. We were able to be totally fluid and to discover physical staging as well as the essence of the play in the rehearsal room. Here the physical staging had to be set.

Once you went into the rehearsal room, how did the challenges change?

The biggest mystery area for me was the puppetry. Three weeks in, I realised I had absolutely not being giving it enough attention, work needed to be done on the narrative, on the acting, and on the staging scene-by-scene. So essentially the puppetry was created and directed by my associate, Aletta Collins, and by the two staff directors, particularly Matt Wilde, and his assistant Dominic Leclerc. They did it, and we were running simultaneous rehearsals virtually the whole time. I was down doing the play scene-by-scene and they were upstairs experimenting with, refining, the puppet world. Then they would turn up in rehearsals and I would see it constantly growing, each puppet becoming more and more like a character. They were delivering to me daemons with whom I could work as if they were actors. It was not me who gave the pine marten all its expressive movements. That was created in another room, between Sam, who plays Pantalaimon, and Aletta and Matt. What I got was a fully functioning pine marten who I could then talk to and make part of the scene.

Have you worked before with that level of delegation?

Yes. It's very different, but I've worked like that with choreographers and also with directors of photography. That's what happens if you are a theatre director and you work in the movies: You ask the director of photography about the mysteries of photography. I'm trying to think of theatre directors currently at work in the English theatre who are fully-fledged geniuses who need to listen to no-one. I'm coming up with almost a blank; Simon McBurney is possibly the only one. We have to be able to collaborate.

As well as the daemons, you had to create physical languages for the bears and the Gallivespians.

The bear heads were the first things to arrive from Michael Curry's workshops which definitely worked. The first prototype daemons didn't. It took a long time to find a prototype daemon that we all liked. Eventually, the pine marten arrived, and when that arrived and we liked it, we had a style for all the daemons. The polar bear head, Michael was very confident about, from the first moment he read the material, and it was brilliant and eminently actable. It took a certain amount of time to discover whether, if you're acting with a bear, you ever talk to the actor or always talk to the head. It transpires that you always talk to the head. There is a strange and rather wonderful dynamic created by the head being the bit that other actors act with, but the actor's face being involved and noble and committed. The Gallivespians were entirely created in-house. The way it worked was that the Curry workshops sent us an array of marvellous things, and then the job was taken over by our own puppet supervisors, headed by David Cauchi. The Gallivespians were created here, and they came late in rehearsals, as did the angels, who were entirely recreated on frameworks sent to us by Michael Curry.

Was Philip Pullman keeping a beady eye on what you were doing throughout?

It was never beady, always extremely supportive. He was a benevolent observer and an occasional very trenchant participant, right through the whole process. I'll give you an example. There are 1300 pages in the books, and six hours on the stage. Things had to go. In the first workshop, and in the very first draft, Mary Malone was there. The Mulefas, the strange wheeled creatures, were never there, and it became very plain that without the Mulefas, Mary Malone was sad and redundant. So, slowly, we came to the conclusion that we had to lose her. It was Philip who said, very simply, "That's fine, but someone has to play the part of the tempter." This was in the course of a discussion at the Studio. As a result of that, the function of the tempter was given to Serafina. It might have been Philip, it might have been Nick (I can never remember these things), who suggested that Serafina in the book has her own story to tell that could, as effectively as Mary Malone's story of the walk on the beach in Portugal, be used, in a different place, to crystalise that relationship of Eve and the tempter. Philip Pullman's attitude always was, "I wrote the story, you are the theatre people. You go ahead and do what you do, and I will occasionally tell you whether I think you're on the wrong track or not."

There are a hundred scenes and a hundred sets. When you moved into the Olivier and started the technical rehearsal, what did you learn about the way you were telling the story?

There was *so* much to do, it was so complex, it required such hard and concentrated work to pull all the elements together, that during the period of technical rehearsal, I lost sight of everything except the need to pull it together. And the thing that made me terribly proud to be part of the National Theatre company was the way that every single department in this theatre was totally focused on pulling this massive thing together so that we could, at the end of the technical rehearsal, run it all through and see what we had. Well, as you know, Part One took five hours, stopped seventeen times and had moments that were dangerously out of control. It took us another twenty-four hours and we were back in control again. It's always the way, with each play, that you lose the play for the time it takes to 'tech' it. You hope that you have it securely enough in the rehearsal room to be able to rediscover it once the tech is done.

We had had very encouraging final run-throughs in the rehearsal room and what we discovered there was secure enough to survive the very exhausting process of putting it together with all this stuff, but it did take three or four performances to play in.

What did you find out from watching an audience watching it?

What we found, and continue to find, is that most people are absorbed, and repeatedly you hear a sound which you always crave in the theatre—silence. It's winter, there are a lot of kids in the house, and that means that the coughing, sneezing and shuffling level is high. What's wonderful though is how, over and over again, it all goes quiet. When you can silence families with flu, you know it's working! I've tried to take a step away from the production and imagine if I knew nothing about this, and someone said "I'm taking you to see a show, it's called *His Dark Materials*". I'd probably sit here and think "This is barking mad." There are undoubtedly certain people who have come under those circumstances and don't get it at all. That's also fine. I don't think we ever want to do things at the National Theatre which are so bland that everybody finds them acceptable.

Is one of the hardest things about being a director to keep looking with a fresh eye at work you've been involved with every day for twelve weeks?

It is. It's very hard. There are some directors I know who come to virtually every performance, but most of us, once it's on, hand it over and come back once every so often to make sure it's not gone absolutely pear-shaped.

The text for these plays has been published, and though it won't be possible for any other theatre to stage it as it is here, it may be that schools and colleges will want to do a production. Do you have any advice for them?

If I was doing it anywhere except here, this big spectacular auditorium with 1,100 seats, if I was doing it in a school hall for an audience of 200, I'd do it with virtually nothing. I think you could announce scenes, if you needed to, or read out stage directions. But I think it's very performable.

Audience questions

The budget for this production is reported as £850,000. If money had been no object, how differently would the production have turned out?

I'm in a very strange position here, because—to use the film analogy again: when you make a movie, the studio decides whether to make the movie and how much to give it, the producer keeps an eye on the budget and makes sure it's not exceeding that budget, and the director is always asking for more money. Well here, I'm all three. It's part of an over-all policy at the National Theatre: what we decided was that in this theatre, the Olivier, we will for the time being devote half the year to simple productions on which we spend very little, so that we can charge very little for the seats. The rest of the year we'll have productions which use all the resources of the theatre and call on all the skills and crafts of the people who work here. This is the National Theatre and we do have the best people, in all departments. So we gave it the kind of budget that you would give a musical. £850,000 is a little more than we spent on *Anything Goes*, and a little less than we spent on *My Fair Lady*. That felt right for two plays, and not so much that we couldn't also make sure that under-eighteens got in at a reasonable price. I don't think I wanted to spend more. I think we spent the right amount.

Would you like to work with puppets more in the future? I come from a country where puppets are used in adult theatre widely and successfully, yet in this country there is no such tradition.

Yes I would, and I would like to have expert puppeteers working here in the future. I would like, and hope, to extend the National's reach to embrace new forms of theatre, new forms of physical and devised theatre, new forms of musical and dance theatre, because I think that's the way the theatre's going. The British theatre has always proudly and strongly been a literary theatre, and the core of the National's work will always be literary, but particularly with the new generation of theatre-makers, it would be wrong for us not to be searching all the time for the best productions in the new forms. It is a wonderful irony that the new forms are very often reinventions of the most ancient forms, which is what puppetry is.

Do you think the books and the play are anti-Church, or specifically anti-Christian? And why has the National found it important to invite the Archbishop of Canterbury to speak at a Platform in March?

We're absolutely delighted that Philip Pullman and the Archbishop will be speaking at a Platform. The thing about these books is that they take our metaphysical needs very seriously. They are not impressed by certain aspects of organised religion, but what they are steeped in is the need to find stories and symbols which explain to us the numinous, that which is beyond our understanding. In other words, it seems to me that the impulse behind these books is very close to a religious impulse. I've never met the Archbishop of Canterbury, but my hunch is that he recognises that impulse in these books and respects it enough to want to discuss with their author the differences between the book's construction of a mythology to answer the religious impulse and Christianity, which those of us who aren't Christians would say, with the deepest respect, is also a highly evolved answer to the human need to explain the numinous. So I think they are not specifically anti-Christian. I think what they *are* is unimpressed by organised religion and what they offer is a series of alternatives to our need to be at one with the numinous.

What was the challenge of capturing the cinematic sweep of the big story and the emotional intensity that Pullman manages to represent so well in the story-telling? How did you find that translated to the stage?

That's one of the challenges and excitements of working in these big theatres, on this big stage. That's exactly what you want—to be able to juxtapose the intense emotion of a mother and a daughter, or two teenagers discovering they love each other, with the big spectacular sweep. That's one of the things that this magnificent stage, with all its original machinery, is able to do.

Did you find directing such a large cast in such varied roles any problem?

I love doing that kind of thing, so it was an absolute joy. It's a tremendous thing to come into rehearsal every day and find 30 people waiting to create stuff together. If you're stuck with one of those exquisite plays for four people, and none of them like each other and you don't like *them*, that can be hard...

2

The Production

David Cauchi Puppet Supervisor
Huw Llewellyn Lighting Department
Sacha Milroy Production Manager
Matt Wilde Staff Director
Olivier Theatre, 8 January 2004

Robert Butler: Sacha, this is one of the biggest productions the National has ever put on, probably the biggest for the last twenty years. In what ways?

Sacha Milroy: The main reason for its scale was that it uses the Olivier's drum revolve, which hadn't been used for quite a few years except as a simple revolve, not in its full capacity. There's an element of the set that sits on top of the drum, which rises and falls. There are approximately 100 scenes over the two plays and almost every scene has a new element of scenery. There are many, many trucks with trees and bits of scenery backstage. There's flying involved too, and there's also a false proscenium which opens in different ways throughout.

Could you tell us about the drum revolve?

SM: Basically it's like a cylinder in two halves. There's a fixed elevator at stage level, and two below. You can bring one of the elevators up to stage level, drop the other, revolve, swap them round, and bring the other one up to stage level. For this show we're using both elevators below stage. On the one that's in the open half, if you see what I mean, there's a very large set which we termed the 'droom' ['drum' and 'room'], it forms a room and the back of it is a projection screen. On the other elevator below the fixed bit of floor, there's a tower which comes up through the floor, and both those elevators can revolve.

How many seconds does it take for a scene to apear?

SM: Eight for the droom to rise six and a half metres.

And with a hundred scenes, it's essential that there's no pause between one scene and the next.

SM: Yes, so the set is nearly always changed below the level of the stage.

Matt, when we met in the summer and were looking at the model, even at that stage, every entrance and exit was being discussed.

Matt Wilde: Yes. Quite often with design, things can evolve in rehearsal that would involve a change to the set, but with this we couldn't just suddenly decide to put a door here or a wall there. The set is so vast and the lead time to get things built was very long, so a lot of the metalwork and the building had to be done in advance. At the beginning of rehearsals we were telling the actors, "You're going to be playing this scene like this, then going off here"; tying them down a bit more than you ordinarily would. It was the only way it could be. But it was a testament to Nick Hytner and Giles Cadle that it could work like that; they had spent so long before we set foot in the the rehearsal room working out how we were going to deliver each scene, each location and each scenario. They were very keen to make sure that as many scenes as possible would end with what in a movie is called 'a wipe'. You'd have a scene going on inside the droom, then you could start another scene on top as the drum revolve descends. So as people are talking, they disappear out of your view, and your eye is taken by another scene which begins as the revolve turns. You constantly have something coming in, you're never waiting, there are no black-outs. It's always on the move, which is part and parcel of how we wanted to tell the story, to keep a constant narrative going.

Was it impossible to change the order of the scenes after a certain point?

SM: Yes. Because the scenery is so complex, it all needed to be choreographed. The scenery was choreographed before we went into the rehearsal room; we had to know which way things went round in order for other things to be set, and if you were setting a scene behind this flat, you had to know what was in front of it. It was very carefully worked out beforehand.

Did you have to plot exactly who would be in each scene, and where they would be?

MW: It wasn't quite as detailed as that, but certainly where the scene was set was plotted. It was still quite malleable. We couldn't make huge changes, but for example, when we got to Bolvangar there was a scene that was originally set inside the canteen, when Lyra meets the kids, and we changed that to an outside scene with the kids skipping and having recreation time. The narrative is still the same but it meant one less change within the drum, and made a much clearer and better scene on the open stage. So the design was still flexible enough to do that.

David, did the puppets start out closer to the style of The Lion King, *which Michael Curry had also designed?*

David Cauchi: There was a workshop back in June with some of the prototype puppets. They were in a *Lion King* style, which was more solid, except for the pine marten, which was more ethereal, secret, more what Nick wanted in terms of the daemons being soul-like. They are mainly made of a wire frame and a type of net which stretches two ways. They can be quite expressive, especially with lights in them. But once we got on stage we found some of them couldn't really be seen.

MW: To try and make sure the daemons had life, we decided that each of them would have a little light inside. In the rehearsal room they worked very beautifully to the eye, but sit them on stage and blast all these lights on them and they disappeared.

Huw, what effect were you after when lighting the daemons?

Huw Llewellyn: There were several ideas to make them look more spiritual, to make them glow, to give them a gentle, spiritual glow. In the end the thing that worked best was to give them a light behind the eyes.

DC: Originally too, they weren't painted as much as they are now, but on stage with the lights on, they had a net curtain look. So we needed to sharpen them up.

SM: And with the size of the Olivier, from the back you couldn't see their features.

MW: Close up they look quite gaudily painted, but the subtlety of their original painting, which was almost like watercolour, washed out completely under the stage lights.

Were a lot of new puppets created in the NT workshops?

DC: Yes. I think we got about 47 from the Curry workshop and there are about 120 in all.

Once rehearsals started, were you in the rehearsal room watching how the actors worked with the daemons?

DC: Yes. For instance, Stelmaria, the snow leopard, was quite a static puppet, and Emily Mytton had quite a bit of trouble trying to manoeuvre it and make it look real. So we made some adjustments to give her a bit more movement.

MW: Yes, Pan was the same, wasn't he? Sam Barnett who plays Pantalaimon, found that just having a handle inside didn't give him enough movement, so you added a small metal attachment on top that gives him more control.

About three weeks into rehearsals there was a run of Part One and it was obvious that a lot of work needed to be done on the daemons. What did you do?

MW: Aletta Collins, who is the choreographer, did the majority of the work, with David and all the puppets, running what we called a Daemon Surgery. Every actor who handled a daemon visited and was asked "How's it going to work? Where's it going to sit?" They had fittings for the mounts, where the daemon is attached. There are knock-on effects on a show this huge—if a mount is to be fitted, the costume department must be told so that a hole can be made, the wigs department needs to know, and so on. Each actor came to the surgery, and a whole process went on to make the daemons work.

What are the things that make daemons come alive?

MW: One of the basic principles of puppetry is that you must never let the puppet die. There should always be something going on. So if you have a bird in your hand, it should never just be a piece of metal and gauze, you must always give it some slight movement. Similarly with the bear heads, they must never just stare, there's always a bit of a twitch. And also, the audience must never lose the eyes of the puppet. As soon as you turn it upstage, you lose the quality of it.

Sacha, were all the sets built outside the National?

SM: No, the majority of the scenery was built in-house, probably the greatest amount of set that's been built in our workshops for a long time. All the trucks, the pieces of scenery on wheels, were built in our carpentry workshop—the houses, the big buoy, the trees. This tree we're sitting under, the one in the Oxford Botanic Garden, took an awfully long time.

What is this tree made of?

SM: There's a metal framework, made by welders.

Then it went through to the props workshop, who did all the carving on the trunk, then they wired on every single little branch, then it went back to the carpentry workshop who built the bench round it, then to the paintshop. There are another nine trees in Trollesund. Again, there's a base, wheels, a metal framework, a polystyrene trunk, foam stuck to it and carved, fir cones stuck on and painted. Those trees were probably in the workshops for six weeks.

Was that the biggest item?

SM: Not the biggest, but probably the most labour intensive. Obviously if you go through sculpting, painting and metalwork, it's a long process. A lot of the set consists of quite simple pieces of scenery, but very beautifully painted. The bigger elements, the pieces of scenery on the drum, represent a huge engineering feat. It's a cantilevered stage, and we used an established scenic engineering firm to make that. It took months and months of discussion. It has a weightload limit of six tons, which includes scenery and people.

What things changed in the course of building the sets?

SM: We modified a few things. We got rid of the laser. We simplified some pieces. The setting for Svalbard was originally a huge carved wall with an upper level and spikes, and the bears were to peer over it. We ended up with much simpler, but very effective, pillars, and we're very glad we did, because there's no way now, we realise, that we could have got it on stage or had anywhere to store it.

At what stage, Huw, did you start on the lighting?

HL: We started in the first days of rehearsals, having a look at this enormous set, which would go from a big open stage showing the Northern Lights, down to small delicate scenes. In the Olivier, we've got more than 1,000 lights, ranging from ones that are two metres long to ones that are a few inches. We had them hidden everywhere: on the roof, in the scenery, under the floor. We have a selection of lights that will change colour, position, pattern. The lamp stays physically in the same position, but the light moves. So we'd start with one light, one colour, one pattern, and it travels across the stage, changing as it goes. For the Northern Lights scene we have a big wrap-around cyclorama and about 45 lights create the effect, which we spent days programming. Each world in the play has its own feel, and it took a while, and a few discussions, to get the right feel.

SM: Huw did a huge amount of research into what was available, what was within budget. The lighting and set were probably the most difficult areas, budget-wise, to rein in.

HL: There was lots of hard-programming. It's all computerised so it can be brought back exactly the same, day after day. We have about 700 individual lighting cues over the two shows, all of which have to be programmed into the lighting board, so they can then be played back for the next performance.

Matt, when you left the rehearsal room and started the technical rehearsal in the theatre, what shocks were in store?

MW: Some things became easier, some more difficult. In the rehearsal room, we had a revolve installed, but it was just a big circle that could go round—not up and down. On stage, there are two revolves: the big drum which goes up and down, and the rim revolve, which goes around the edge. They can go in the same direction, or counter to each other. On a lot of the journeys the actors make, particularly when Lyra and the Gyptians are walking through the northern snows, they are walking counter to the other revolve. They didn't have that in the rehearsal room, so the first time they encountered huge trees coming towards them, for instance, was in the tech. They also felt for the first time the sensation of being up on top of the drum revolve. It's easy in the rehearsal room to say, "This scene will be happening up there on the drum", and the actors say "Yeah, yeah". But then you get to the tech, suddenly they realise how high up they are. All those things are terribly exciting, but also very time-consuming, because you have to work out how they get to each new area safely, how they come down at speed, how fast things move.

Did you make changes to what you had rehearsed?

MW: Not many really. This huge piece we call the 'portcullis', which comes down and has panels, doorways in it, we had none of this in rehearsal, so some things had to be changed when we got on stage. Someone would be exiting and realise they couldn't go that way because there was a tree coming. Quite often in the rehearsal room, an actor would wander off upstage and you would remind them they couldn't because the portcullis would be there.

Were there times when actors found themselves down there when they needed to be up here?

MW: There were a few times when people missed the boat. Once, when it was Mrs Coulter's entrance, she didn't appear, and the message came that she'd been locked in the droom down below, because once you go down in the revolve, the doors are locked for safety reasons. So we did lose actors a couple of times.

SM: But there were only a few times when scene changes took longer than we thought they would.

MW: There was one bit where Will and Lyra go back from Cittàgazze to Oxford to get the alethiometer from Lord Boreal's. They were on top of the 'droom', as it corkscrewed up, and they were looking down from the roof. They simply ran out of lines before it got there, so Nick Wright wrote a few more.

SM: It just took a lot longer than any of us had anticipated to get through the technical. This space could be incredibly dangerous, the potential for disaster is huge, so we really did have to take it at quite a slow pace.

And there's a whole other company back there, isn't there?

SM: There are 24 stage crew, eight electricians, four sound, ten dressers, two wigs, and so on. And there's actually no time when there isn't a scene change about to happen, so they're moving stuff around behind the portcullis, preparing the next scene. As soon as the drum goes down, there are eight people down below who change the scenery and the furniture.

MW: In the rehearsal room, where all we had was a revolve, when we started to run the play, people would run on with chairs and tables in the scene changes, and even that seemed like madness. But when we got in here and had to push on a 20-foot hut and huge pieces of machinery—it's a whole play in itself.

Since the previews, have there been changes in the design?

SM: We carried on work on the lighting for quite a while. What always happens in a situation like this is that the lighting time gets compressed, so we needed time to perfect it.

HL: And some things changed as the actors got used to the space and we found different places where we could use effects, or stars, or dry ice.

MW: The video changed quite a lot, too. The tech was the first time we could see what the video would look like on this screen. They just slowly kept adding bits and pieces to it.

SM: There are three video projectors in the droom, and the one image is made up from three projectors. It looks very simple but took weeks and weeks.

Audience questions

I'd be interested to know how you did the children's daemons, when they change shape.

MW: In the books, they change rapidly. There's no way we could deliver that so swiftly and so constantly, but we knew we had to do it a couple of times to set up the notion that until you reach adolescence, your daemon doesn't settle into one shape. So we needed a few key moments, when it changed from one to another, with Lyra's daemon, Pantalaimon, in particular. There were a few moments when he came on as a pine marten, then he's a wildcat, then a mouse. We do it by simple sleight of hand. There's a sequence right at the beginning when the puppeteers are sat behind Lyra and Roger. As the action is going on above their heads, they take a mouse from behind their backs, the mouse runs away, they catch it and pass it back to the puppeteer, and out comes another shape. Trying to keep it very simple, not to be too clever, but just to set up the notion that it is constantly changing. It was easier with Lyra because she could go off with a pine marten and come back with a muskrat, or something.

If the lighting changes and the video are programmed, how does all that stay in sequence with the actors?

SM: There's a deputy stage manager [Lesley Walmsley or Kerry McDevitt] who sits in a box at the back of the stalls, with a headset on, and she is linked to the sound operator, the video operator, the flyman, the automation person, the stage manager on stage, in fact to all the different departments. She has a copy of the script, and all the cues are written in it—when they happen, and on what line the actor is speaking. That's how it's all co-ordinated. But this is a very difficult show because there are cues happening all the time.

MW: Probably one of the most complicated ones is when Will cuts the window. He's stood looking out there, there's music that accompanies the sound effect, and a sound effect that accompanies the cutting. On a huge screen behind him, you see the entrance he has cut open to reveal Oxford. He has to look out here, and it's all done with cue lights.

Do you think the use of the drum revolve in His Dark Materials *is more ambitious than what has been done before? I remember seeing it used in* The Wind in the Willows.

SM: It probably is, with the use of the rim revolve and the sliders and the portcullis and the amount of other things going on with it. The drum revolve has been used before quite extensively, but I think the combination of ways we've used it is unique.

HL: There's more scenery down there than there was for *The Wind in the Willows*, but it was the same principle of a room inside the drum. I think *The Shaughraun* used a much larger single piece travelling up and down and revolving, but this is certainly more complicated once you're down there.

*Is there anything in the production you'd like to have done
differently?*

MW: Once you hand it over to the actors, they always
find new things, but there always comes a time on every
production when you have to say let's stop fiddling. I think
most of us are really thrilled with what we've achieved, and
it tells a great story.

How do you cope with shadows, in the lighting?

HL: Where possible we try to get rid of them. We didn't
completely eliminate them, but sometimes that gives a very
nice effect.

*If you have 700 lighting cues, how many cues in all are
called in the duration of the show?*

HL: There are cues for the rim revolve, the elevators,
the actors, the musicians, sound cues, flying cues… There
must be well over a thousand.

And does the DSM give them all?

SM: Yes, she never stops talking!

What kind of background research did you do?

MW: For the daemons, lots of animal videos were
watched. Something that's wonderful about this is that
there's only a certain amount of research you *can* do
because it's about imagination. Who knows what happens
when you blast through the Aurora and go into another
world? Nobody!

SM: Giles, the designer, and Nick, the director, discussed it for at least a year, and then the other parts of the
creative team came in, and tied into that.

*My wife and I have been to the theatre three times a week for
the last 25 years, we've seen every show that's ever been at the*

*National Theatre. We were away on holiday when booking
opened for this, and when we got back we couldn't get a seat,
and the box office told me for the first time in 25 years to come
and queue. I got on the first underground train, and I was
number two in the queue. And I was delighted because it
was a Saturday and we saw both shows in one day. The
complexity of what you four have explained is incredible.
I was thrilled with the talk yesterday, as well, and I was
so pleased to hear the production is coming back next year.
Every child from five to a hundred and five should see it.*

3

The Author

Philip Pullman
Olivier Theatre, 9 January 2004

Robert Butler: I first went to speak to Philip in the autumn of last year, and I asked him if staging His Dark Materials *was an impossible task. He said nothing was impossible in the theatre, but it was going to be very difficult. My first question is—how well do you think it's been done?*

Philip Pullman: About as well as it could possibly be done. The resources in a place like this are second to none; the talent available here is astonishing. I feel as if my story has fallen into the best possible hands to make a dramatic production out of something which was conceived to exist between the page and the mind of the reader, which is a very different thing, of course, from doing something that you know is going to be public eventually. There's a lot of stuff which is 'interior' in the book. There's one section which had to be cut entirely because it consists of a woman scientist called Mary Malone, who isn't in the stage version at all, describing her thinking, discovering and wondering about this mysterious thing I call 'Dust'. You can't show that on stage, it's not inherently dramatic. An example of something which *is* dramatic, which helped me get the book started, is the first four words in the story: *Lyra and her daemon.* I began the first book with the idea of the girl going into a room, hiding, and overhearing something she isn't supposed to hear, and it all comes out of that. But to get her in there I found very difficult. On the face of it, all you have to do is say, "She went through the hall, into the room, she heard someone coming, and she hid in the wardrobe." But it was not easy to do that and to tell the readers what was going on in her mind; you would have had to say, "She thought this, she felt that, she wondered so-and-so". That's not nearly as interesting as it is when you've got another voice involved. I was stuck for several weeks, until I discovered she had this daemon. As soon as I wrote *Lyra and her daemon...* instantly it becomes a dialogue. She can say "Let's go in here", he can say "No, you mustn't", and she can say "Oh come on, don't be a coward". It's inherently dramatic. That's the sort of thing that works on the stage, but not all the book is like that, so I wasn't sure how it would work. But I'm thrilled with what they've done.

The story on stage has different emphases. Is that all right?

Well, there have to be, because one thing a novel can do is take you directly into the mind of a character, you can tell people what they're thinking. And of course, there's another thing, which the novel has in common with the cinema, and which isn't available to the stage—the close-up. You can see a little message being passed from hand to hand, tiny details which you can't see from way up at the back of the circle. You have to give a different emphasis to it, to arrange the story, the scenes, so that every important bit of it is visible from way, way up. That's stage-craft, not novel-craft.

Are there themes which emerge more strongly in the stage production, and others which have moved more into the background?

Yes, inevitably there are, because you have to cut five-sixths of what's there, which is in fact what's happened. To read the whole thing aloud, as I know because I recorded the audio book, takes thirty-five hours; the stage plays are six hours, so five-sixths had to go. It would have had to go whoever did it, but the other thing that comes into play here is the mind of the person who's writing the play. Nicholas Wright's take on it is very much his take; another playwright would have perhaps chosen slightly different incidents, seen it from a different point of view, given a different emotional tonality to the thing.

For instance, does the Church emerge more strongly, and in darker colours, in the plays?

I think it probably does, yes, but that's partly because these are dramatic scenes, things you can see vividly, strong personalities clashing with each other, face to face. Those dramatic things work very well on stage, so perhaps that comes out more vividly, or is more salient in the plays.

Some of the ecological themes, for example, aren't as prominent.

That's probably true, yes. For instance the character of Mary Malone, the scientist, who looks at things scientifically and wonders why the world she finds herself in has developed like this rather than like that. These are internal reflective debates and have to bear on the ecology of that world. I was rather sorry not to see on stage the creatures with wheels that she meets, but that's something that it wasn't possible to show.

What was your role in the production?

It wasn't a formal one. I was invited, very kindly, to come and see the original workshops. I saw early drafts of Nicholas Wright's script, and that was very interesting indeed. I saw it again at a later stage when it was fully cast and the script was finalised, and watching it take shape here on the stage was fascinating. I've been very warmly welcomed, and a couple of small suggestions I've made about an emphasis here or there have been taken up without any hesitation. I felt welcome all the time, it wasn't something I felt I was intruding on.

There were one or two points where you felt aspects of the story had to be retained. For instance, if Mary Malone didn't exist, there was still an important event that needed to happen.

This has to do with functions in the story. Things happen in the story not for arbitrary reasons but because they lead on to something else or because they have a meaning within the emotional line of the whole story. What Mary Malone exists for, in a sense, is to tell a story to Lyra, a story about falling in love. In so doing, she gives Lyra the means of expressing something she herself doesn't yet know she feels. That was very important, it had to happen, and if Mary isn't there, who can do it? I can't remember who it was who thought that the function should devolve on Serafina Pekkala, but it was a very good choice. In effect, in a curious way, this bit of the story is about Cinderella. Mary Malone at that point (Serafina Pekkala in the stage version) does what the Fairy Godmother did for Cinderella: helping her take the next stage, as it were, in the journey towards maturity.

A member of the audience, before this talk, asked if I would ask you if there was any element of this production that you would like to have included in the books?

Yes, certainly. I had Lyra and Will arrange to meet, in their different worlds, in the Botanic Garden at midday. It's *much* much better at midnight. I wish I'd thought of that. There's no-one around, it's more romantic.

Before you became a writer, you were a teacher and taught children about Will and Lyra's age. Is there something very particular about twelve-year-olds?

Not about twelve-year-olds rather than thirteen-year-olds or eleven-year-olds. It's that this period falls right in the middle of the stage when we are changing, probably as radically as we ever do. It's that part of our lives when we discover that we have a soul, a mind, a personality of our own rather than the one formed by our families. It sometimes occurs to me that your life begins when you are born, but your life *story* begins at that moment when you discover that you are in the wrong family by mistake. You define yourself the only way you can, in relation to the people around you, and you think "Who are these horrible people I have to live with? They're embarrassing, their taste in music is appalling, I hate to bring my friends home because I'm embarrassed by what they might say." That's adolescence, when you are discovering who you are, your body is changing and you're becoming a sexual being. It's embarrassing and a source of self-consciousness, and of all sorts of feelings and ideas you can't understand. It's also when we begin to discover things outside ourselves for the first time—intellectual things, poetry or science or art. It's the most vivid and exciting age. So it was very interesting to teach children who were just beginning to make that radical change.

Did you worry about the age of the actors playing these parts?

Well, I did wonder about that, until I heard Nicholas Wright's wonderful idea for starting the plays. It's brilliant to start with Will and Lyra later on, the age that the two actors are, coming back in their two different worlds and talking to each other and across each other. That establishes who they are, the fact that these are the two people we're going to be with throughout the story, and then when the scene revolves and we go back in the story, we accept it. We accept that Anna in her twenties is playing Lyra at the age of twelve.

When Lyra reads the alethiometer and Will uses the subtle knife, they rely on non-rational thought or peripheral, intuitive vision. Is one of the aspects of your book an attack, in a way, on over-rational thinking?

That would be grossly simplifying it. No, I'm not attacking rational thinking, I'm pointing out that there are other forms of thinking in the world. I couldn't possibly attack rational thinking. It's given us the scientific method, electricity and explanations for the world we live in. Of course rational thinking is fundamentally important but it isn't the only means of apprehending the world. There is a state of mind that you enter when you read the alethiometer or use the subtle knife, or when you write poetry. The best description of this is Keats's, in one of his letters: "Negative capability, that is when a man is capable of being in uncertainties, mysteries, doubts, without any irritable reaching after fact and reason." It's a very difficult one to persuade people about. It's very important if you're going to do anything creative, to discover anything or write about anything. It's no good straining after it because it doesn't come if you strain for it. You have to relax into it, and that's difficult to do unless you're comfortable with being in twilight, and many people aren't.

Is that something the great Eastern philosophies are more attuned to?

I don't think only Eastern philosophies. We've talked about Keats, and Wordsworth also talks about the sense almost of sinking into a trance in front of nature. It's a state of mind where you become aware of shadows and things moving about in the mist, as it were. If you look at them directly, they vanish, so you've got to be prepared to look away and be happy with not knowing fully what these things are going on around you. That's what it's like. I think every poet, novelist and dramatist, perhaps every scientist, is familiar with this state.

What kind of twelve-year-old were you?

Intensely romantic. I used to fall in love all the time. Something that happened when I was twelve years old has always struck me as an example of good teaching. This happened on a rainy afternoon in my secondary school. For some reason, our teacher was away, so the class I was in was sitting in the hall while the teacher of another class was rehearsing the choir. The rain stopped and the sun came out and the sunbeams shone through the windows and lit up someone on the other side of the hall. The music teacher didn't explain what they were playing, and I didn't know what it was then, but I've since learnt that it was the aria 'Voi che sapete' from Mozart's *Marriage of Figaro*. The combination of hearing this music and the sunlight striking through the windows onto a particular girl—well, I was lost. Oddly enough the music is about adolescent yearning. But what was good about that was that the teacher didn't say "This is what this music is about, this is what the words mean, it's in the key of whatever..." No explanation at all, you just come across it and it affects you more profoundly and powerfully than you can ever imagine; then it's gone. It's mysterious. The same thing happened a year or so later in another class, when a teacher was rehearsing some kids in choral speaking. They were doing 'The Journey of the Magi'. He didn't explain to us what it was, just had the kids rehearsing, and suddenly, these words "A cold coming they had of it..." These words, without any explanation burnt themselves into my heart. It was extraordinary. So that's the sort of child I was.

You seem to have had immense freedom as a child in the Welsh hills.

Well, those were the days before paedophiles! You weren't worried about horrible men waiting behind every bush. And there wasn't any traffic up in the Welsh hills, so there was nothing to be afraid of and we could run over the hills all day long. So we did, and we wandered on the beach, and came back in time for supper. It was wonderful freedom. That is something that our children today sadly miss. The world seems to have grown more dangerous, to us who are parents, so we don't allow our children the enormous beneficial freedom that we used to have—buying fireworks from the shop and setting them off on the roof of the toilets. Mustn't do it, very bad, very wrong! But you should see them running out...

In the plays, science is represented by Dr Sargent, and the science is used for the wrong ends.

Anything can be used for the wrong ends. Things are used for the wrong ends when they are divorced from a sense of who we fully are. When we have a sense of who we fully are and the world we fully belong to, you tend to get things right on the whole because then you see yourself in a moral perspective, in a moral context, in a moral connection with the rest of the universe. It's when you feel yourself isolated from that and think "I'm above all that, I'm in some isolated, superior bubble", that's when things go wrong.

And institutions can encourage this.

Institutions can justify what they do by referring to moral absolutes, invisible absolutes. This is my quarrel with organised religion, not that it's about God, but that it's about morality. My quarrel would be exactly the same with Soviet Russia, for example, an explicitly atheist state which nevertheless worked in exactly the same way as a religion. You had a holy book; you had prophets who brought the word (Marx and Lenin and so on); you had a priesthood, the Communist Party, which was above the normal rules; you had a view of history which tended towards a great Millennial vision of peace and plenty; you had a whole apparatus of denunciation, confession and show trial and punishment which was exactly like the Spanish Inquisition; you even had holy relics preserved—all the apparatus of an institutional religion. Here was a way of organising society which referred to absolutes for its justification rather than to ordinary human experience.

There were some Christians who were very upset at your depiction of the church. One of the first things they say is that Jesus isn't mentioned.

No. I think I'm going to have to get round to Jesus, somewhere. We'll see what happens in the next book, *The Book of Dust*. In the scheme of things that underpins the writing, Jesus would be one of these great prophets, great religious geniuses whose teaching is too revolutionary, too difficult, too hard to live up to, and so is perverted and altered and controlled and led into safe channels by the human organisation which is set up in his name.

When the Authority dies in the book, would it be right to say that he is a symbol and people with religious beliefs need to find a new symbol?

That's exactly right. In the book, and this is one of the things you can't show on stage, when Lyra and Will lift the dying Authority up, he's like paper, he's just made of words, just an idea. What is dying in that scene is an old idea of God, and he dies with a sigh "of the most profound and exhausted relief."

The German mystic, Meister Eckhart, said the way to find God was to take leave of God.

That idea probably has the same kind of root, yes.

Your books are translated into 30 languages; they must be read in countries where they have a very different view of life after death and of the World of the Dead. How are your books received there?

I don't know. I don't get many Korean reviews. It's an odd process because all you know about it is when you hear from your agent that you've got an offer from the Faroes, or somewhere. You sign a contract and get a tiny cheque, then eighteen months later a book arrives that you can't read, and that's all you know about it. I hope that the story itself, as I've tried to tell it in the books, is understandable on its own terms. You don't have to know much about classical mythology, for example, to feel what's going on when Lyra and Will go to the World of the Dead. I think that's fairly self-explanatory.

The play text is published, and although this production can't move to any other theatre, as it's so tied up with the technical staging here, would it be possible for it to be staged in different ways, as a school production for instance?

Yes, it could. It could be done in all sorts of ways. You'd have to find different ways of staging it, that's all. One of the great merits of this script is its swiftness, it moves so quickly. The joy of watching the stage move around is because it helps that swiftness. Nothing that happens on the stage is here for its own sake; it's all for the story. If the scene moves around it's because we're moving to another place and it happens at once, there isn't a second wasted. That's wonderful story-telling, and you could do that with nothing, I guess. It would be interesting to see. But the swiftness is the thing. If someone got it into their heads to bring on a set, pull a curtain, laboriously pull that set off and bring on another, it would go on all week, wouldn't it?

Audience questions

How do you feel when you hear His Dark Materials *described simply as children's books?*

They were published originally as children's books because they were published by a children's publisher. I've always felt this was a great help. If they'd been published by an adult publisher, they would have been called fantasy and would have gone on fantasy shelves with all the mock-Tolkiens and what-have-you, and the majority of adults who have read them would never have seen them. Adults know what they like, and if you know you don't like fantasy you won't pick it up. Adults who have read these books have done so because their children have persuaded them, and they found it enjoyable and told their friends, so I've found a much wider readership than I would have if it had been published as an adult book. So I'm very happy for it to be called a children's book.

Is there going to be a film?

There are plans to make three films, yes. There's a script for the first part, but the next stage is to find a director and go through all that process. That hasn't happened yet, as far as I know. I can't say more because that's all I know.

Where did you get that line from: "and she walked into the sky"?

That's actually an Alexandrine, that last line of *Northern Lights*. It's often the case that I find myself aware of the rhythm of the next sentence before I know the content. I have to write in silence for that reason. I can't write with music playing because the music gets in the way. I knew I wanted to end the book with an Alexandrine (I think I'm right in saying that it is), and that fitted, but it's quite a good last line. I was quite pleased with it.

What is it that enthrals you most about a story?

The sense of desperate longing to know what happens next. That's what I love in all sorts of stories, whether they are fairy tales or thrillers or great novels. One of the most exciting reading experiences I've ever had was standing at a bus stop in Oxford, not unlike the one that appears on this stage, reading the last few chapters of Jane Austen's *Persuasion*. I was desperate to know what was going to happen, how it was all going to end up. I missed two buses! That's not the only thing of course, but that for me is pretty fundamental.

When a child is born in Lyra's world, where does the daemon come from? Does it come out with the baby?

I haven't made a great study of the gynaecology in Lyra's world. The answer is that I don't know. I don't know because I didn't have to write a scene in which anyone was born. If I had, I would have had to think about it. But it's a good question.

Which book did you like writing the most?

I don't really think of them as three separate things, to me they have always been one long story. They were published as three separate books because it made publishing sense, bookselling sense, economic sense and so on; also because the story fell naturally into three parts, but I never thought of them as three separate stories, so I can't say which is my favourite. There are some passages which I really enjoyed writing. From the first moment I thought of Will, I knew that there would have to be a moment when he meets Iorek, the bear. I wanted that to be a dramatic passage, very exciting and full of tension, and I looked forward to that and enjoyed writing that passage.

Was there something that you read over and over again as a child, which had an impact?

I can't say I read the Bible assiduously, but I was brought up with the Bible because my grandfather was a clergyman and I spent a lot of time in his household and went to church every Sunday, so the words of the King James Bible and the words of the 1662 *Book of Common Prayer* and of *Hymns Ancient and Modern*, some of which I quote at the beginning of *The Amber Spyglass*—'O tell of his might, O sing of his grace'—they were very important to me, not only because of what they said but because of the rhythm of the words, the thunderous power and majesty of the language. Another book which I read over and over again, and loved, was a book called *The Magic Pudding* by Norman Lindsay, an Australian children's classic. It's the funniest children's book ever written, a wonderful book.

What would your daemon be?

This is a question I have been asked once or twice before. I'd like to have a daemon that was photogenic. (Isn't it odd, they don't make camera lenses out of the same glass they make mirrors out of, do they?) But you can't choose your daemon, as Lyra discovers in the first book, in a passage which had to be lost from the play. She's talking to the old sailor and she says "Why do daemons have to settle?" He says, "They always have done." She says, "What if it settles in a form you don't like?" And he says, "You've just got to put up with it, haven't you? Plenty of folk would like to have a lion as a daemon and they end up with a poodle." So you can't really choose, but based on the way I work and the way things are, I suppose my daemon would probably be a magpie or a jackdaw, or one of those birds that steal bright things, which is what storytellers do. It's the brightness that matters, not the intrinsic value; a diamond or a KitKat wrapper, it's all the same to me if it glitters and shines. I'm just as happy to steal from *Neighbours* as I am from Shakespeare. So probably a jackdaw.

Will the science in your books make science more accessible in general?

I hope, if not the science itself, then the scientific *attitude*, which I take to be one of curiosity and wonder and openness towards the world, as depicted by Mary Malone. I was careful to get the science as correct as I could; I read as widely as I had time for. But it's quite easy to find out about science these days, there's a lot of wonderful popular science writing about, and it's thrilling to find out about quantum theory, string theory, all that sort of stuff— absolutely entrancing. I put as much of it in the books as I thought the story needed, because I think if you put too much research into a book it becomes inert, sits there on the page not moving. The function of research, for a writer of fiction, is not to enable you to put it undigested in the book but to give you the confidence to make up more stuff when you need it. So I read sufficient to enable me to do that.

I was quite startled, when I saw the play, that Mrs Coulter and Lord Asriel didn't sacrifice themselves for Lyra. I would be very interested to know what you felt about that.

This is something that might be emphasised a different way if a different playwright had done the adaptation. The story is refracted, if you like, through the prism of Nicholas Wright's personality. There was a technical problem on this stage, since abysses generally go down and you can't literally hurl yourself down because broken necks might result.

I'd like to know where you get your inspiration from?

I don't know where it comes *from*, but I know where it comes *to*. It comes to my desk. If I'm not there, it goes away again.

Because people's daemons become settled around the age of thirteen, does that mean we have no more hope of change? Am I doomed to remain this person?

Yes, 'fraid so. You're stuck with it. Actually, that's a source of strength as well, as Lyra will discover. Knowing what sort of person you are is a great help to knowing what you can do and making the best of yourself. I sometimes think it would be a great help if we did know what our daemons were because we wouldn't waste time trying to do things beyond our powers or not within our nature. Once, on a book tour of the United States, I was in a book store in Seattle, and someone came up to me and said, "Why do daemons have to settle? *My* daemon hasn't settled! I don't *want* my daemon to settle! He's not going to settle!" She was a woman in her forties and she was wearing little white ankle socks and had her hair in bunches.

At the end of the story you have an angel telling the

children that there are other ways to travel between the worlds. What did you mean by that?

What I meant by that was imagination, really. It's that state of mind again—the state of mind in which Lyra can read the alethiometer and Will can use the subtle knife. In that state of mind you can perceive other things, perhaps other worlds.

Which character were you most proud of writing?

I hope I'm not proud; that's not a helpful state of mind for a writer because then you think you're wonderful and you don't cross anything out. The character I *enjoyed* most was Mrs Coulter, and I enjoyed her because I never knew what she was going to do next. She shocked me to my very marrow. When I had a Mrs Coulter scene coming up, I had to be very diplomatic, almost bring her a bunch of flowers beforehand. "Mrs Coulter, we've got this scene in a cave now, but it's a nice cave. There's a great part for you, you'll enjoy it." But I always enjoyed Mrs Coulter scenes because she was far more ruthless than I would ever be; she did things I wouldn't dare to do.

When will your next book be out?

The next book will be quite different. It's a fairytale called *The Scarecrow and His Servant*, and that comes out at the end of this year. Actually, the idea for that book first struck me when I was sitting over there in the Olivier Stalls, watching, on this very stage, Bernstein's *Candide*.

Has the cast of the play equalled your imagination of the characters?

Oh yes, more so. It's been as good as and better than I could ever have hoped. It's a strange thing seeing people you've imagined take physical shape; it shuts down some possibilities and opens many others, in each case. But it's a wonderful cast. It's such a thrill to hear my words, as changed and added to by Nicholas Wright, given voice by these wonderful actors.

4

The Adapter

Nicholas Wright
Olivier Theatre, 20 January 2004

*Robert Butler: Did your childhood in South Africa
correspond in any way to that of Lyra and Will?*

Nicholas Wright: Well, it was similar to Lyra's in that I had
an absent father, who in my case didn't appear till I was five.
I thought about that a lot when I was adapting the books.
And my childhood was also a little like Will's because I was a
loner. In a very sporting and racist society, I didn't fit in. I
was stagestruck, in love with the theatre from the moment
I knew that such a thing existed.

Did you live in a town?

We lived in Cape Town—a little English colonial town.

Why didn't you meet your father till you were five?

Because he was fighting World War Two and had somehow managed not to come home until victory was
declared. My mother and my grandmother took me to the
station to meet him. A train came in with a lot of men in
khaki looking out and waving, while my mother and lots of
other mothers walked up and down the platform. I remember quite distinctly watching my mother peering at the
train windows; I was under the impression that she was
choosing one of the soldiers, rather than looking for one
that she might recognise. I remember getting very agitated
because she was taking so long to make up her mind and
I knew from experience of shopping with her that if she
didn't do so pretty soon, we would be left with a soldier
that nobody else wanted. This was what I understood to
have happened when she brought one of them home. It
was a peculiar start to my relationship with my father and
not very conducive to our getting on very well. My mother
told me many years later that I pulled her aside and asked
her why she'd chosen one with a moustache.

How did you get into acting?

Through the radio. Because I'd been completely spoiled as a small child, I could read very well from a very early age. Some people came to the school to look for small children who could act in a radio play. They gave me a script and I could read it easily. So that led to my doing hundreds of broadcasts, from the age of about six. Then I got chosen by a marvellous and, in her day, very famous actress called Gwen Ffrangcon-Davies, who was living in Cape Town. She auditioned me to act with her in a play based on *The Turn of the Screw* by Henry James, in which I had to play Miles, the angelic but possibly deeply corrupt little boy. And I also had a puppet company which we used to take round to children's parties and do shows for money.

What sort of puppets were they?

We used to make them, and also buy them from England. And we made our own scenery. To this day, I can watch any amount of bad acting, and actually quite like it, but bad puppetry upsets me terribly. It was a huge joy, in the preparation for *His Dark Materials,* to see the incredible care and skill which the actors all took in using the puppets. If you've seen the show you'll know what I mean—the puppets are really alive, they're so subtle and so nuanced; they never jiggle about in a meaningless way, they're always giving a thought-out performance, which is what a puppet has to do. Then I came to England and went to drama school and what had happened—which was like Lyra and the alethiometer, though I had never realised it until this moment—was that in going through puberty I'd completely lost my childlike ability to act. Something that had seemed so natural when I was a little boy, I could no longer do. I spent the next part of my life, up to when I started to write, looking for something I could do in the theatre; I had a great love for theatre, but I needed to find a talent that I could actually give to it.

What happened to your ability to act? As you got older, did you become self-conscious?

You become aware of what you're doing, and so lose the ability to do it spontaneously. It's exactly like that Kleist story, 'On the Marionette Theatre', which Philip Pullman has said was so important to the thinking behind *His Dark Materials.* As soon as you're aware of it, all the spontaneity goes and you start watching yourself. You can, if you have talent, learn to do it again, perhaps better than you could before, but it's a slow process of piecing it all together. As a child actor, you learn the words, you speak up, and stand up straight and everybody thinks you're absolutely marvellous. It's nothing to do with acting at all.

This is one of the most important themes of the play, isn't it?

There are so many themes in the books, and one has to look for the overriding one that develops through them. For me, the overwhelming central theme was first Lyra's and then Will's journey into growing up, the experience of growing up and becoming aware of the opposite sex, becoming aware that your parents are not always what you think they are, that they're not always going to be there. So much of what happens, particularly in the second play, is that the figures who seem strong and resourceful and will always be there for you and support you, start to fall away, or you start to see them as mortal, fallible, or old, and more and more to realise that you're on your own.

*When you were the NT's literary manager, were you
always looking for plays for young people, and were there
always plenty of plays out there?*

When I was literary manager here, I always thought
there should be a play for young people in the repertoire at
any one time. Obviously it would not always be a major
production like this one, but even if it were in the after-
noons or on Saturday mornings, that should be a stream
that never stopped. And that never happened. It was, in
policy terms, a bit sporadic, more sporadic than it should
have been. Of course there's a huge grey area—for a child
of twelve, many adult plays are absolutely delightful and
incredibly interesting; it's hard to draw a barrier. When we
were creating *His Dark Materials*, we always thought that it
was for twelve-year-olds upwards and I think that was a little bit conservative. Some people would always say, "Yes,
but my ten-year-old is quite old enough to come and see
it." And in fact I've seen children of five, six, and seven in
the audience who are absolutely rapt, completely held by
it, to my surprise, because we never had that young an
audience in mind. It just happened, and seems to work for
them, which is fantastic.

*I understand you read the books as they were being
published —*

I read *Northern Lights* and *The Subtle Knife* together, just
as *The Amber Spyglass* was coming out; and then I read
that. That was a little bit before the National had decided
to do the plays, which I think was about two and a half
years ago.

*It's often said that the novels looked impossible to stage.
What made you think they might make a play?*

Nothing at all, to tell you the truth. I'd read the books and loved them, then Nick Hytner asked me if I had read them, and I talked about how wonderful I thought they were. Then later he rang and said they'd finally negotiated the rights to turn them into a play, and would I do it? I said, absolutely. I knew that they would be difficult to adapt, though I didn't, at that time, know what the difficulties would be. For example, the thing people always ask, and the first thing Nick and I talked about, was how do you do the daemons? Now that that problem has been solved, I think very successfully, it seems no longer a problem. What was difficult, really, was the multiplicity of Philip's stories, the way in which stories come into the foreground, move into the background, characters totally disappear, or the narrative follows one character for quite a long time. To abridge it so that the story still made sense and to meld all the seams together so that the whole play—not just one strand of it—seemed to be moving forward at the same time, that was really hard, it was the hardest thing I've ever done.

You've written your own plays, written screenplays and adapted plays for the stage, but have you ever adapted a novel for the stage before?

No, I don't think I have. I've done quite a lot for television and for film but they've always been infinitely simpler than this. The easiest novel to adapt for the stage would be a 60-page novella like *The Turn of the Screw*.

When Robert Bolt wrote the screenplay for Dr Zhivago, *he said he read the novel twice, made a list of the ten most important points and didn't look at the novel again. You did the opposite, really, staying very close for as long as possible.*

I did stay close. One of the first things I did was to go to Oxford and look for the tree which is the first thing you see on stage in this adaptation, and which, with the bench around it, is a pretty exact replica of a tree and a bench in the Botanic Garden. It's not actually the tree and the bench which Philip Pullman imagined Will and Lyra sitting on; that is a straight bench. But I saw this one, and took a photograph of it. I thought it would be so beautiful to have a round bench on stage. I wrote a synopsis of the books, and then did lots of synopses of the plays as I thought they would work out. Then we did a three-week workshop with all the creative team: director, designer, choreographer. We made a lot of decisions then about how the daemons would be done, what they would look like, what the important themes were. Then I wrote another full draft, and we did a reading over a couple of days. I wrote another draft; we did another workshop, this time for two weeks. And each time characters fell away—Mary Malone fell away, Lee Scoresby's life was sadly truncated—things like that happened.

What were the early decisions you took?

A very early decision was how to divide the second book so that three books would become two plays. We knew where the division would come, but how to ensure that the first play didn't feel as though it had ended two thirds of the way through—a lot of work went into that. When *The Subtle Knife* opens, you lose Lyra completely and have this new character called Will who you've never met before. You can't do that on stage just by sticking the two things together; it would feel 'broken-backed'.

Did you think about what genre you would be working in, whether it would be drama, tragedy, tragi-comedy?

Yes, we thought about that a lot. It's an epic, which practically nobody writes these days. It has the epic form—a myth which stands for birth, growing up and finally death. It's a great big arc like *The Mystery Plays*, like *The Ring Cycle*, which actually it often reminds me of. So it's an epic but has a human scale. You have characters who are partly hugely larger than life, almost god-like, but at the same time their conflicts are intensely reminiscent of the conflicts you have in a normal family, there's a domestic side to them. It reminded me very much of some of the plays of Ibsen, which I love, where the characters are enormous and are all the time living within great conflict, conflicts which matter to them. This is very important I think about *His Dark Materials*, books and plays. There's nothing trivial about their concerns at all. Their concerns are the vast ones of life and death and the important things. That was the kind of play that ran around in my head. I often thought of Ibsen's *John Gabriel Borkman*, where people ascend an enormous mountain and address the cosmos, yet at the same time their emotions are real and domestic and to do with the relationships that are closest to them. They never fly off into fantasy. They are always intensely real.

Because this is such a huge production, there must have been a time when the order of the scenes had to be fixed.

I think it was about last June, before rehearsals began, that the design was essentially completed. After that point I really couldn't change the sequence of scenes or what those scenes were. I could change what people said in those scenes, because that had no technical knock-on, but I couldn't say "This isn't going to be a ship now, it's going to be a snowy waste", because the design was already locked off.

There's another aspect too, which you won't and shouldn't be aware of when you see the play. Each scene is not just a scene; it's also an opportunity for another scene to be prepared out of sight. There's a great deal more happening backstage than there is before your eyes. That affects things like the length of scenes. Sometimes there are little short scenes between scenes. These should have proper dramatic value, but they are also the opportunity for something to be changed within the stage machinery. There were certainly times when I'd have to write a scene in a particular way to fit this technical marvel beneath our feet, which is making the whole thing work—the Olivier drum-revolve. It's a bit like the old-fashioned front-cloth scenes, when a painted canvas would come down and a scene would be played in front of it while stagehands went bump-bump-bump behind. Just in terms of the script, it's a bit like that: large-scale scenes are interspersed with more intimate ones.

As you were writing these various drafts, what kind of input did Philip Pullman have?

Little, but crucial. He was having a crazy year, when the fame of the books was taking off. Nick and I met him at a very early stage, and I think he just made a decision to trust us and left us alone for great stretches. He came to each of the workshops for some time, kept in touch with the scripts, and every so often would make some point with extraordinary precision and force and sensitivity. I think at every stage we took his points, which were never, ever, to do with making it more like the book. He never, ever said that. At one stage he suggested a change because he thought it would be more like Lyra, and he was right. Otherwise he always said "I think the play would be better if you did so-

and-so." He was completely generous in that way, and I really admire that because the disciplines of a novel— particularly a vast, capacious, three-part novel of the kind he'd written—and of a play are so different that a lot had to be changed. He understood that right from the word go.

While you were working on the stage play of His Dark Materials, *Tom Stoppard was working on the screenplay, and at the same time his play* Jumpers *was being revived at the National. Did you ever meet and talk about the impossible tasks you'd set yourselves?*

We talked a bit, very early on, when we were both starting work. We would run into each other by chance, and as I recall, in those days we were quite forthcoming with each other. As time went by we became more and more friendly but more and more reticent at the same time. It was a bit like when one's mother exchanges recipes with a friend while leaving out important ingredients. I think we didn't want to know what the other was doing; we each had enough to think about. So I haven't the faintest idea what his screenplay is like, and I don't know whether he's been to see the plays.

When rehearsals started, how did the script change?

I did quite a lot of rewrites in rehearsal, a lot of the kind of stuff you have to do to clarify the story. Characters changed a bit, Lord Roke ended up saying a lot more than he had originally...

Did you find that once, say, Anna Maxwell Martin started rehearsing the role of Lyra, that led you towards writing lines for her?

Yes, of course you subsume the character as the actor produces that character. I found it interesting that as

Dominic's performance took shape, Will's way of talking changed a little. Will's overriding imperative is to be invisible. As he explains, he's done it all his life. His family has no money because his mother is on her own and seems incapable of earning a living; there's a small army pension, no doubt. He can only be going to the local comprehensive, and that means he's going to talk like all the other boys. He can't afford to sound posh, he must adopt the camouflage of being a little below his father's social class, his father being an army officer. I followed this in the writing, which I think was right. He's right as he's written in the books and right in the plays, but doesn't speak in quite the same way. That's one way in which the performance shaped the writing.

It's going to be impossible for these plays to be done anywhere else with the kind of production values you have in the Olivier, but you have said that the script of His Dark Materials *would make an excellent school play.*

Oh, yes, I think so. If you're doing it for 1,100 people, as here, you have an obligation to throw into it all the resources that a theatre like the National can. But if you're doing it in the school hall you can do it in a different way, with nothing at all. Usually when you write a play you think maybe it could go into the West End or Broadway or something, but there's no way that this play could do anything like that. No other theatre could hold it. It's written for this stage machinery and for this wonderful, all-encompassing auditorium.

If I was a drama teacher, what advice would you give me about how to stage this play?

The important thing is that you don't stop the story to move things around between scenes. I think you'd say to the kids, "Read the books, and come back and show us how you're going to do these daemons, or angels, or flying witches." Just do it through imagination.

Audience questions

I didn't quite understand how the last scene of Part Two related back to the first scene of Part One.

For those who haven't seen the plays, there's a framing device, which is used very sparingly. At the beginning, Will and Lyra are about the same age as the actors who play them, Anna and Dominic, and they're sitting next to each other, in different worlds, as they've said they will do once a year. In the book, they meet at noon, but partly for technical reasons, in the play they meet at night. Because the play lasts six hours, we're assuming that they meet at midnight and stay there until dawn, which in summer could reasonably take about six hours. So the scene under the tree at the end is the end of the scene that starts at the very beginning of the play.

RB: I should say that, when I interviewed Philip Pullman and asked him if there was anything from the stage adaptation that he wished he'd had in his books, he said, "I wish I'd set the scene in the Botanic Garden at night. It's much better because no-one else would be around."

A playwright friend of mine, when she read that scene, and Will says "I had a job climbing over the wall", said "But they're going to meet for the rest of their lives. What will happen when they're eighty!"

But isn't Lyra wearing a different costume in that scene at the end of Part Two?

Well spotted! They're not wearing the clothes they were wearing in the first scene, but that's because there isn't time for the actors to change.

What did happen to Lee Scoresby's plot? Was his whole story in the script originally? Did you think about cutting him altogether, like Mary Malone.

I think for about two drafts his whole story was there— the shoot-out, the lot. We didn't cut him completely because we liked him so much. Now he fulfils the first half of the role he has in the books, but not the second half. It's a shame because it's a wonderful story. Lee starts off as a cynic who's just doing it for the money, but ends up giving up his life for Lyra.

In the book Lyra's parents give up their lives for Lyra and you've changed that. Why is that?

In the books, for those who don't know them, Lord Asriel is waging war against the Authority who is a kind of God-figure, but we discover in the course of the books that the Authority is no longer the supreme power, that there is a power behind the throne, far more important than the Authority, who is an archangel called Metatron. In the books Lord Asriel and Mrs Coulter fall into the abyss while entrapping Metatron, thereby ridding the world of him and saving Lyra and Will and their worlds from the threat of this cruel despot. We lost Metatron, partly because it was very hard to imagine how we would actually stage him. So I have changed that and the Metatron danger in the play is now what Lord Asriel sees in himself: it is his own inclination to despotism, his own pride, his own cruelty, that he destroys. That is a brief description of the struggle, the complex train of thought that led to this.

Did the fact that there were so many titanic themes put you off undertaking the project at all?

No, not at all. A lot of plays aren't about anything at all, certainly not about anything that really matters. So I thought it was fantastic to be doing a play about great and timeless issues. What is death like? What is guilt like? What is it like to completely reassess your whole view of the world, your view of your parents? I thought all those things were fantastic. The theme of death is irresistible, which is what it all really finally leads up to.

Did you use any of the dialogue from the books?

Yes, I started off using a lot, then, a little like Robert Bolt with *Dr Zhivago*, for the last six months I did very little going back to the books. There are speeches that I know are in the books, but if you ask me what proportion, I couldn't tell you. And of course I've also sometimes given one character's speeches to another. A wonderful speech by a character called King Ogunwe, who doesn't exist in the plays, is now given to Mrs Coulter. And I don't know if any of you remember a very likeable character called Ma Costa who tells Lyra the true story of her parentage. Well that story is in the first play, in a much briefer form, but in the mouth of a character who is one of her parents.

Could you give an example of a suggestion Philip Pullman made to the adaptation?

His suggestions were very practical, and very theatrical. For example, towards the end of the first half of the second play, the Gallivespians, little flying creatures, sting Mrs Coulter and immobilise her, thereby rescuing Lyra. At a run-through, Philip said that we didn't know they were stinging her, because we hadn't said anything about the sting before, and that was absolutely right. This had the result that we inserted some lines a few moments earlier when the lethal quality of the Gallivespian sting was referred to. It sounds small, but it turns a moment which would be mystifying into something clear.

There's a scene between Will and the bears about which he said "That scene doesn't have the tension it should, I can't think why." Then he said, "Oh, I see what's wrong. Will issues the challenge to Iorek, the king bear. Will says 'If you win, you can eat me'. But what's the other half? What if Will wins?" And I realised he was absolutely right, if Will wins the challenge, the bears have to drop what they're doing, come with him, defend him and fight for him. That way there's a win/lose balance each way. So you see they're not huge things, but they're very dramaturgically expert.

RB: But there was the big suggestion Philip Pullman made about Mary Malone's role—

Oh, yes, this is a big one. When we cut the character of Mary Malone, Philip said, "That's fine, but you've lost something important about the books, which is the theme of temptation, and temptation through storytelling." It's the telling of a story that awakens Will and Lyra to the beginnings of adult sexuality. Nick Hytner said, "I know what we can do, Serafina can carry that theme forward." Then I came in and said, "We have a story which I've been looking for a place for..." There's a beautiful story which Serafina tells about her love affair with Farder Coram many years earlier. She could tell that story to Lyra earlier on. And Philip said, "Yes, and a reprise of the story about the fruit can lead into the temptation". So it was an extraordinarily important thing he suggested, which led to Serafina carrying the weight of that crucial theme from the books, and that's how it came into the plays.

5

The Conversation

Philip Pullman
Dr Rowan Williams Archbishop of Canterbury
Olivier Theatre, 15 March 2004

Robert Butler: About six months ago, and on the very first day of rehearsals for His Dark Materials, *Philip Pullman had to leave the rehearsal room to go down to Lambeth Palace to record an interview with the Archbishop of Canterbury, Dr Rowan Williams. It was later broadcast on Channel 4. In that conversation they discussed the crisis in childhood, whether it existed, whether or not it was fuelled by consumerism and by the media, and what space could be found for children and for childhood.*

Tonight they're going to continue this conversation, but moving on to other areas, in particular religious education, and the representation of religion in drama and entertainment. Last Monday the Archbishop spoke at Downing Street about His Dark Materials *and he recommended it, saying he was delighted to see large school parties in the audience and he found it vastly encouraging. But he did say that he hoped teachers were equipped to tease out what in Pullman's world is and is not reflective of Christian teaching as Christians understand it.*

I would like to start the conversation by asking the Archbishop how we might tease out the differences.

Dr Rowan Williams: I suppose one of the questions I would like to hear more about from Philip is what has happened to Jesus in the church in this world [of *His Dark Materials*], because one of the interesting things for me, in the model of the church in the plays and the books, is that it's a church, as it were, without redemption. It's entirely about control. And although I know that's how a lot of people do see the church, you won't be surprised to know that

that's not exactly how I see it. Chance would be a fine thing! There is also the other question which I raised last week about the fascinating figure of The Authority in the books and the plays, who is God for all practical purposes in lots of people's eyes, yet of course is not the Creator. Those are the kinds of differences that I am intrigued by here.

Philip Pullman: Well, to answer the question about Jesus first: no, he doesn't figure in the teaching of the church, as I describe the church in the story. I think he's mentioned once, in the context of this notion of wisdom that works secretly and quietly, not in the great courts and palaces of the earth, but among ordinary people. There are some teachers who have embodied this quality, but whose teaching has perhaps been perverted or twisted, and been used in a fashion that they themselves didn't either desire or expect or could see happening.

There's a sort of reference to the teaching of Jesus, which I may return to in the next book—but I don't want to anticipate too much because I've found that if I tell people what I'm going to write about, something happens to prevent it. But I'm conscious that this is a question that has been hovering over people's understanding of the story.

The figure of The Authority is rather easier. In the sort of creation myth that underlies *His Dark Materials*, which is never fully explicit but which I was discovering as I was writing it, the notion is that there never was a Creator. Instead there was matter, and this matter gradually became conscious of itself and developed Dust. Dust proceeds from matter as a way of understanding itself. The Authority was the first figure that condensed, as it were, in this way; and from then on he was the oldest, the most powerful, the most authoritative. All the other angels at first believed he was the Creator and then some angels decided that he wasn't, and so we had the temptation and the Fall etc—all that sort of stuff came from that.

The Authority, who dies in the story is, well, one of the metaphors I use. In the passage I wrote describing his death, he was as light as paper—in other words, he has a reality which is only symbolic. And the last expression on his face is that of "profound and exhausted relief". That was important for me, but it's not something you can easily show to the back of a theatre, through a puppet.

RW: That's very helpful because I think it reinforces my sense that part of the mythology here came from some of those early Jewish and Christian or half-Christian versions of the story in which there is a terrific drama of cosmic revolt. The underlying theme is that someone is trying to pull the wool over your eyes, and wisdom is an unmasking. I think if you have a view of God which makes God internal to the universe, that's what happens.

PP: Yes.

RW: Someone will be pulling the wool over your eyes?

PP: I suppose that's right, yes. The word that covers some of these early creation narratives is gnostic—the Gnostic heresy, as it became once Christianity was defined. The idea that the world we live in, the physical universe, is actually a false thing, made by a false God, and the true God, our true home, our true spiritual home is infinitely distant, far off, a long, long way away from that. This sense is something we find a lot of in popular culture, don't you think? In things like *The X-Files*—"the truth is out there", and *The Matrix*. Everything we see is the false creation of some wicked power that, as you say, is trying to pull the wool over our eyes.

Can I just ask you a question? What do you put this down to? The great salience of gnostic feelings, gnostic sentiments and ways of thinking in our present world? What's the source of that, do you think?

RW: Well, let me try two thoughts on that. One is that the human sense that things are not in harmony, not on track, can very easily lead you into a kind of dramatic or even melodramatic picture of the universe in which somebody's got to be blamed. So, "we was robbed", you know, "we have been deceived"; it should have been different, it could have been different. Salvation, or whatever you want to call it, then becomes very much a matter of getting out from underneath the falsehood, pulling away the masks, and that's tremendously powerful I think, as a myth of liberation.

It's what a lot of people feel is owed to them, and I think some of the fascination of the Enlightenment itself, as a moment in cultural history, is of being able to say we can do without authority because authority is always after us. One 20th-century philosopher said that the attraction of somebody like Freud is charm. It is charming to destroy prejudice, because we have the sense that this is the real story. Now we've got it.

The second thing about the popularity of this mythology is that even the most secularised person very often has problems about the meaning of the body. It is very tempting, very charming again I think, very attractive to say, what really matters is my will. If the reality is my will and my thoughts, and if there is somewhere a condition where

I can get the body where it belongs, get it under control, then that's where I want to be. And, of course, Christians and other religious people do buy into that in ways that are very problematic. It's very hard sometimes to get the balance right theologically.

PP: Well, this brings up the Fall of course, or the notions of sin that are bound up with our physicality, supposedly, which is one thing I was trying to get away from in my story. I try to present the idea that the Fall, like any myth, is not something that has happened once in a historical sense but something that happens again and again in all our lives. The Fall is something that happens to all of us when we move from childhood through adolescence to adulthood and I wanted to find a way of presenting it as something natural and good, to be welcomed and celebrated, rather than deplored.

RW: There's a real tension I think in quite a lot of Christian thinking about just that question. Is the Fall about bodies or not? You do get some Christian thinkers who would say, yes, even the body is the result of the Fall, and others who say, well no, it has a metaphorical sense, and there is a level of bodily existence, which is OK, which is willed by God.

Coincidentally I was reading, just a few days ago, a letter by David Jones, the Anglo-Welsh poet and painter. He's writing about the Fall and Milton's perception of it and he notes that in Milton, as soon as Adam and Eve are thrown out of Eden, the first thing they do is to have sex. David Jones says "that is the bloody limit" because he's writing as a Catholic with a rather strong investment in the idea of saved material life. There is a right, a godly way of this existing—it's not just about experience, sex, the body and so forth, being part of what goes wrong. It's a mixed bag historically.

PP: One of the most interesting things for me about the notion of the Fall, is that the first thing that happened to Adam and Eve was that, with consciousness, they were embarrassed. For me it's all bound up with consciousness, the coming of understanding of things, and the beginning of intellectual enquiry. Things which happen typically in one's adolescence, when one begins to be interested in poetry and art and science and all these other things. With consciousness comes self-consciousness, comes shame, comes embarrassment, comes all these things which are very difficult to deal with.

RW: That's right. As a religious person, I would say that's a neutral phenomenon. That's just what happens, and one of the fallacies of religion that's not working is to suppose that somehow you can spin the wheel backwards, and go back to pure unself-consciousness.

PP: Which is a mis-reading because, after all, it says in Genesis, there's an angel with a fiery sword standing in the way. You can't go back.

RW: Can't go back. The only way is forward. Yes, and sorry to quote Anglo-Welsh poets again, but one of R S Thomas's pieces is about there being no way back to the Garden. The only way is forward to whatever there is. I think I quoted to you once before, when we were talking about this, the statement of Von Hugel, the Catholic philosopher at the beginning of the last century, who says the greatest good for an unfallen being would be innocence, but the greatest good for a fallen being is forgiveness and reconciliation, which sort of brings in what I think the version you're getting at leaves out.

PP: I think that's probably right. Now, how do we teach this? What do we teach in RE?

RW: Not enough I think. That was really the burden of what I was trying to drive at last week in the Downing Street talk. I'm worried about a religious education that tries to do it from the outside in, which says, "Look here's what religious people do", which is always just a little bit on the edge of "here are these funny foreigners doing strange things".

I've seen some RE text books which do give you that rather uncomfortable impression that you're looking from outside. "Ooh, isn't that interesting?" And that doesn't really give you much sense of what it feels like to be religious, why it's difficult to be religious, why it hurts to be religious, why people want to stop being religious, and why people want to start being religious. One of the ways you can do this is by personal narrative, which is why I'm interested in the role of fiction and autobiography in religious education.

PP: Yes. Yes. Now, if one of the goals of RE is to help children understand what it feels like to be religious, are there different ways of being religious? Does it feel different for example to be a Sikh than it does to be a Christian? And if so, shall we help children feel all these different ways?

RW: It's a tall order isn't it? But I think obviously there are differences unless what you want to say is that what matters is the religiousness and never mind the details— which I think is a dead end, frankly. Even people who've been rather critical of what I've said on religious education have, I think, on the whole agreed that that's not the way to go. There's a limit to the empathy you can expect of somebody who's still learning, exploring at that level, but I don't want to underrate the seriousness of students in schools, and what they can cope with.

PP: I'm completely with you on that one.

RW: I want to try and help people to see why, as I say, religious belief can be difficult, why it can be appallingly oppressive, why it can be amazingly liberating at times. To get inside that a bit. That's why I've talked about autobiography as a vehicle for this, looking at what people actually say about how it's difficult and how they live through it, or don't. Then I think you've begun to see that being religious is a way of being human at a certain depth. I don't think you'd entirely disagree with that, from what I hear, even if you don't think it's finally about anything solid.

PP: Well, I think religion is something that all people, people in every society, have done. It's a universal human impulse: the sense of awe and transcendence. It's possible to find that in most societies, and in a great deal of art. And this brings me on to what I was going to ask next. How do you see fiction for example?

RW: Being used in…?

PP: Would you use fiction? Would you, be sort of instrumental about it? Or is it an end in itself? I rather think fiction's an end in itself.

RW: I would use it in teaching, but I think one's got to be very careful about using it, in the sense of saying, well you've got to have a message you can squeeze out.

PP: Well, this is what worries me.

RW: What you learn, I think, after absorbing a really serious piece of fiction, is not a message. Your world has expanded, your world has enlarged at the end of it, and the more a writer focuses on message, the less expansion there'll be. I think that's why sometimes the most successful, "Christian" fiction is written by people who are not trying hard to be Christian about it. A bit of a paradox, but I'm thinking of Flannery O'Connor, the American writer, as my favourite example here. She's somebody who, quite deliberately, doesn't set out to make the points that you might expect her to be making, but wants to build a world in which certain things may become plausible, or tangible, palpable, but not to get a message across.

PP: Isn't this what happens, though, when we read fiction, any sort of fiction, sympathetically? Good fiction, classic fiction; good art of any sort in fact?

RW: Yes, and I think that's why. Yes.

PP: We're looking for an enlargement of imaginative sympathy, aren't we?

RW: That's right. We're looking for a sense that our present definitions of what it is to be human—what it is to live in the world—are not necessarily the last word or the exhaustive version of reality, and that the truth is out there in another sense. It's out there in a bigger universe.

PP: Well, the truth is in the library, perhaps.

RW: I suppose it has to do, perhaps, with some of those characteristically religious themes like absolution (how you live with the past), with the possibilities of forgiveness, and with whatever it is that poses at depth the question of how I relate to my entire environment—not just to what's immediately around me, but to my entire environment—which, of course, for a religious person, has God as the ultimate shape around it.

PP: Yes. Do you think fiction and drama and poetry—you mentioned all these three things—do you think they work in different ways? From my point of view, probably, the one of these that is least able to present a religious point of view is drama and the one that is most likely to be able to do it successfully is poetry.

RW: Why is drama the least?

PP: Because the sort of experience that we're talking about, is a private, solitary, internal one, isn't it?

RW: No, not really. I'm not sure I buy that.

PP: I don't want to use just my story to hog the argument, but there's a passage in *His Dark Materials*, when Mary Malone is on her own, wondering and speculating about the nature of this mysterious thing that she's investigating, this thing I call Dust. Now it's a very important passage in the book, but you couldn't show it on stage because all it would consist of is a woman, sitting in a tree, thinking.

RW: Yes, I see that. On the other hand, drama is an extremely communal activity. It is something which is necessarily about human interaction...

PP: Well, it's about human beings relating to each other, isn't it?

RW: That's right—the origins of Western drama are actually ritual and religious, in ways that still surface rather surprisingly. And the kind of event that living theatre is, is, I think, still very ritualised. And I mean that in a good sense: so that it's bound to be a place where certain emotions and perceptions are allowed out, literally, to roam the stage in a corporate environment. It may be inimical to religion interpreted as you have, as solitary wrestling with problems, but what about those themes of corporate purgation, crisis?

PP: Well, you're absolutely right about that, I remember seeing on this very stage the great production of the *Oresteia* 20 years ago, or whenever it was, and the sense of, yes, corporate, social coming together and understanding of how to deal with these terrible events and terrible feelings. It's a ritual way of dealing with them that satisfies us aesthetically, morally, emotionally and in every other sort of way. Oh yes, I agree with you about that. But the solitary experience —what Wordsworth was talking about for example in 'Tintern Abbey', something like that—that perhaps is a sort of religious experience which can't be dramatised.

RW: That I suppose underlines the fact that religious experience is not one thing. There are lots of things going on: different kinds of artistic activity—or artistic representation—do the job in different contexts for different people. Certainly what Wordsworth was talking about is essentially a moment of, in the benign sense, self-awareness. A real awareness of being a person in a living context—being bound up with something immense—that runs through his individual awareness. But there are other things, I think, that religious experience is about. I've spoken about reconciliation, and that I think is something that is harder to do in poetry.

PP: Because you need a story?

RW: You need a story and dramatic interaction.

RB: *One form we haven't discussed is film, which works mainly in a very realistic way in representing religious stories. Do you find that a useful approach?*

RW: Works in a very realistic way—do you think so?

RB: *You're encouraged to think you're actually there, and it's not working, as the theatre does, through metaphor.*

RW: I think film is deeply metaphorical and I think that, actually, the last thing film does, is to represent what's there. To me, it's about the creation of a particular visual sequence—highly patterned, highly stylised. Some directors, of course, are much more overt about that than others. It's animated icons rather than representation. Things don't happen like that.

But, if all art is moving reality into another medium—remaking reality, you might almost say—film is no exception. I'm actually very interested in how film does deal with the religious issues, and I'm not talking here about religious films which are often slightly depressing, simply as art works.

My favourite film with a sort of religious subtext is *Babette's Feast*, and there's not very much doctrine in that, not very much overt religiosity, except the rather grim religiosity of the old people of the village and their piteous circle. It tells the story of a sort of secular saviour, who has spent all she has on equipping the people of the village to have an elaborate, pointless, over-the-top feast, in the course of which, sins are confessed and reconciliation is achieved. It's a sort of bloated version of a short story. It's not a realistic depiction of rural life in Denmark, and it's not the film itself that's making a religious point. But watching it, and absorbing what I call the animated icon of it, gives me all sorts of things to reflect on in my own belief system. None of it is realistic, that's not what it's for.

The mistake made by some religious films, the sort of 1950s biblical epic stuff, is to think, well we have got to show religious things happening and we all know what religious things are like—they have soft music and a kind of glow around the edges. That's I think why I find it a bit depressing, because it's actually very difficult (and maybe this does pick up on the drama thing again) to represent religious experience in any context. There's always been that kind of wrestling and tension about it, can it be shown? And that's where the easy resolution of something like *The Robe* or *The Ten Commandments* really won't do. What that sort of film shows is simply a kind of projection of a religiously tinged emotionalism. It doesn't show things changing—that's the hard thing.

PP: Which leads us to Mel Gibson. Have you seen his film—*The Passion of the Christ*?

RW: I haven't seen it.

PP: Nor have I, so we can talk about it! That's all right.

RW: We're allowed opinions without the constraints of reality!

RB: *He is presumably selling his film on the basis that it is very realistic. I mean people are thinking that they're getting close to seeing what happened.*

PP: What fascinates me about the phenomenon, is that churches apparently are spending thousands of pounds on block booking tickets and giving them away to atheists in the hope that by seeing someone tortured to death we'll reform.

RW: It's a real concern I think because—I don't mean atheists reforming, though that'd be nice!—the question of how you represent what Christians believe is the pivotal event in the history of the universe is no simple one and I don't think can ever be answered.

PP: But I thought the pivotal event was the Resurrection which doesn't come in [to *The Passion*].

RW: The pivotal event is not just the Resurrection but the whole of that Easter complex, if you like, which is why a realistic representation of the crucifixion on its own won't say what has to be said. Curiously, along the history of the church, the way it's been done in the church's liturgy and art very often doesn't seem very realistic in that sense. You walk through the experience of Holy Week, from Palm Sunday to Easter Sunday, in a sort of ritual way: picking up a bit of the gospels here, a bit of the prophets and the psalms there; performing certain ritual acts (in the Catholic tradition particularly); watching through the night; participating in a very curious and distinctive liturgy for Good Friday, with the bare cross being brought in and unveiled. All of that is an attempt to say what a mere recitation of the story, or a mere photograph, couldn't say.

I remember years ago somebody saying to me that, given the choice between having a video of the Sermon on the Mount, and having half an hour with St. Peter after his betrayal, he'd go for the latter because you would see in the complexities, the changes, the tensions, that Peter had undergone—something you wouldn't see just on a video of the sermon—which would land you back in all the problems of what would you really see there, what would you really hear.

PP: This is exactly the heart of the problem of representation isn't it, whether we're talking about a myth or something else. I'm very struck by Karen Armstrong's description in her new book of the difference between *myth*, which she calls something that is a basic human response to the problems of the great questions of life and death, and what she calls *logos*, the rational attempt to work out answers by using our reason. Now, a rational depiction of the events of Holy Week would have to be a sort of cinema.

You'd have to show it cinematically, as I take it that Mel Gibson does. But that would miss the other part wouldn't it? Wouldn't it miss the mythical element of it, which is something that has to be lived and lived and lived again?

RW: That's right.

PP: As an atheist I'm rather on difficult ground here, but presumably this is what a Christian believes.

RW: Yes.

PP: That it is something whose truth is not historical only but has a truth that also sort of lives on. Is that right?

RW: Absolutely right, and it's a pity that the word mythology has the negative overtones that it has.

PP: That's right because it has connotations of "it's only a myth, it's not true", but that's not really what a myth is.

RW: We are, at least, talking about a set of historical events which have, as I would say by God's guidance, become the centre of a vastly complex, imaginative scheme in which the whole of human history and human life gets reorientated. It is shown, liturgically, dramatically, artistically, in ways that constantly transgress those apparently realistic modes. It's interesting that Mel Gibson does pick up one or two of these things in the film. The medieval convention is that you show the skull of Adam at the foot of the cross, so the blood runs down on to the skull of Adam— I don't actually imagine that the skull of Adam was on the historical Calvary. In fact, I'd be very surprised indeed. But that is a deeply mythological moment.

PP: But doesn't the audience have to *know* that it is the skull of Adam? It doesn't come with a label saying "Adam's skull, look". So this depends on a sort of shared knowledge?

RW: It depends on a sort of induction into how it all works. Likewise, I was going to mention, in the Eastern Orthodox church, how do you show the resurrection? Well you can't actually, because if you try to show Jesus rising from the tomb, you end up with some of those rather embarrassingly awful Renaissance pictures of a sort of luminous figure bouncing out of the tomb on clouds and lots of people sitting around looking rather surprised. In the Orthodox church what you do is you show Jesus in Hell, rescuing Adam and Eve, standing astraddle a great pit, and grabbing Adam and Eve, pulling them out of their tombs. Again, you need to know what's going on, but what that's saying is, that this kind of event is really not going to be represented at all effectively, at all adequately, by an attempted pseudo-photography.

PP: It's the difference between myth and something that's to be understood literally. Karen Armstrong goes on to make the point that the split between these two forms of understanding, has resulted in the unfortunate phenomenon of fundamentalism, where you get people trying to read a mythical account as if it is a literal account. It says God created the world in six days, it must have been six days, like that. And so you have creation science taught at that school in Gateshead, which is deplorable.

RW: The curious thing about fundamentalism is, I think, that it's a very, very modern phenomenon. It's a kind of reaction to a scientistic rationalism which says, "It couldn't have been like that". The fundamentalist, instead of saying, "Well, what question's being asked here?", immediately bounces back and says, "Oh yes it was", and you then have a sterile stand-off, which doesn't at all get to the level of the mythological and the proper positive sense that you're talking about.

Audience Questions

Why was the Archbishop recently dismissive about the teaching of humanism in secondary schools?

RW: I hope I wasn't dismissive; perhaps I was, and if so, I'm sorry. The point I was trying to make was that atheism and humanism are not, if you like, free standing systems. That to understand what's going on you need to understand a bit about what they're reacting against religiously, I would say. And therefore to begin with a proper internalised understanding of how religions work and why they're different is how you get into understanding atheism and humanism.

Is one person's religious truth someone else's lie, and does that inevitably lead to warfare?

PP: This raises the question of relativism and so on. It's a terribly difficult one. If my religion is true, does that mean your religion is false, or are we worshipping the same god by different names? I'm temperamentally 'agin' the post-modernist position that there is no truth and it depends on where you are and it's all a result of the capitalist, imperialist hegemony of bourgeois… all this sort of stuff. I'm agin that, but I couldn't tell you why. I'm rather like the old preacher who was 'agin sin'. That was the message that came from his sermon. It's a temperamental, visceral thing.

RW: There is a real question as to whether we come at this in a sort of binary way—whether the question is always either completely true or completely false, and that I think is what provokes violence between points of view. I don't believe, let's say, the Buddhist is right about the way the universe is. On the other hand I think I would be a far stupider person even than I am if I couldn't recognise that Buddhists know things that as a Christian I need to learn. Even if I believe my basic Christian view is as it is.

Can you please say, Dr Williams, why you think it is the business of schools to teach children what it is to be religious, especially when there are so many competing types of religion?

RW: A clarification perhaps: I don't think it's the business of schools in general to inculcate a particular set of religious beliefs—church schools are another matter—but I don't think that's the job of religious education in the state school. But I believe it's important, indeed essential, to teach religion in the sense that, as Philip said, this is something that human beings do. They do it in ways which dramatically extend, challenge and complicate their humanity. Try and pull that out and you actually have an education that is something, I would say, less than human.

Now how you steer that through, as you say, the shark infested waters of controversy between religions—and indeed, for heaven's sake, within religions—I don't entirely know. But I think it can be done if you keep before you very clearly that sense that (well, if you believe this is right, and I do) that religion is something without which human beings are not what they might be.

A question from a fellow atheist who is appalled by the materialism of this society: how would Philip Pullman recommend children develop a spiritual life?

PP: I don't use the word spiritual myself, because I don't have a clear sense of what it means. But I think it depends on your view of education: whether you think that the true end and purpose of education is to help children grow up, compete and face the economic challenges of the global environment we're going to face in the 21st century, or whether you think it's to do with helping them see that they are the true heirs and inheritors of the riches—the philosophical, the artistic, the scientific, the literary riches— of the whole world. Do you believe in setting children's minds alive and ablaze with excitement and passion or is it a matter of filling them with facts and testing them on them? It depends on your vision of education—and I know which one I'd go for.

RW: I think we're entirely at one on that, I must say.

Is the relationship between Christianity and fiction perhaps that Christianity itself is a story, and is about incarnation?

RW: Yes, I think there's a lot of truth in that, that you can't communicate Christianity simply as a set of ideas. At some point you're going to have to sit down and tell a story. And tell a story which, because it's a story, is bound to have some loose ends, some awkwardnesses. As it is we have four versions of the story of Jesus in the New Testament, because of that sense that a story can always be retold. And that introduces a bit of irony in the narrative, which is very important in reinforcing the sense that this is something mysterious. I think there is something in that fundamental characteristic of Christianity which helps to enable a particular kind of storytelling.

PP: Story is fundamental. We began with Jesus. We might as well end by reminding ourselves that Jesus was one of the greatest storytellers there's ever been. Whether or not he was the Son of God, he was a great storyteller.

RW [laughing]: Eight out of ten!

6

The Actors

Dominic Cooper
Anna Maxwell Martin
Olivier Theatre, 20 March 2004

*Robert Butler: As anyone who has seen His Dark
Materials will know, it's a huge production, running for
six hours with over a hundred scenes, but the whole thing
depends on the two central characters and how strongly
they affect the audience and carry us along with them.
This production's success relies to an enormous extent
on the two actors in conversation this evening—Anna
Maxwell Martin, who plays Lyra, and Dominic Cooper,
who plays Will.*

*I'd like to start by asking them how they approach a
character that has started in a book, a character that many
members of the audience already know about?*

Anna Maxwell Martin: My first reaction was panic. It's
very different from doing a normal play where you glean
what you can from the script and form a character that way.
With this we had three books in front of us, describing in
minute detail what a character felt and thought from beginning to end. So I read the books and thought about the
character, and then it was about going back to the play and
thinking about the through-line of the character in the play,
which is very different from the book. And there are things
which aren't in the play of course. In the first few weeks I
found it quite hard having to give up things I'd become
attached to about Lyra from the book, little nuances that
just couldn't be done in the play, where you have to move
character and story-telling along really quickly.

What sort of things did you give up?

AMM: I can't remember! When you start to form a
character it's so detailed, it fills your head so much, but at
some point that all goes and you just play it.

Could you explain what you mean by a through-line? Is it that you're not playing one single character but a lot of different shades?

AMM: You have to be firmly established in what your character is about, how they think and feel, how they relate to every single person they come across. Once you know all that stuff and it's in your head—it's quite complicated—you sort of have to let it go. Then you find the through-line of the character, the journey they go on and how that journey affects them. I think, thanks to Philip Pullman, and to Nicholas Wright's adaptation, it's actually quite easy to find the through-line for Lyra. I never consciously thought "I've got to make her seem more grown-up now" because the way she reacts to things in the plays make that quite clear.

Dominic, did you go back to the books?

Dominic Cooper: Yes, often. I remember it was really terrifying to approach a character everyone knows so well. We started the workshops, over a year and a half ago, and I remember seeing Philip for the first time. We were putting something together on stage. It was very basic, the daemons were just socks on our hands, and we were running round doing bits of dialogue, and suddenly seeing the man who had written these characters and had known them in his head for the last ten years, was one of the most terrifying moments of my life. You just didn't know what you were doing at that stage. But if you ever got stuck, you could always refer to the books, there's such a wealth of information there.

Did you go back to the book for each scene?

AMM: Yes, if ever you think "Why am I doing this? Why am I reacting like that?" you can go back to the book and you know it's all there.

Even though what happened in the book was sometimes different from the play?

AMM: The thing I found most difficult, up until a couple of weeks ago, was the moment in the play where Mrs Coulter and Lord Asriel and Will and Lyra all meet up at the end. That never happens in the books, so to know how Lyra would react to that was really hard. I don't think I really realised it until recently. Sometimes that happens, it takes you a long time to get somewhere. I always realised that her destiny was Will, or that was how she felt, but these ideal parents she so hoped for... I think at that point she thinks "Actually I don't need you, you're not what I want." But moments like that are huge for anyone.

DC: These two characters, Lyra and Will, have the most specific, clear through-lines in the story. I think it was more difficult for many of the other characters, who have been cut or reduced substantially, to make their stories clear.

How did your sense of Will change through rehearsals? Did you know on day one how you were going to play him?

DC: No, not at all. I think it changed with *our* interaction, when we started behaving like a couple of ten-year-olds in the rehearsal room. That was good. We didn't really have time to work very thoroughly at the beginning. I remember Nick saying that it was going to be like a military campaign because of how technical it is. We had to find those moments ourselves, in the scenes. Cittàgazze for example was a really wonderful moment because it was one point where we sat down together and had a scene, chatted, rather than running around the stage trying to kill green monsters.

AMM: When we started there really was a sense that it had to be got through, had to be blocked, and there was very little time to sit down and discuss things. I remember Dominic and I went for a coffee a few weeks into rehearsal; we discussed our scenes, and went through a lot of decisions, but there hadn't been time…

What sort of decisions?

DC: I suppose just what they're feeling at different moments, how their relationship has progressed and how they feel about one another at different points. We just went through all the scenes in the book to see where they were at that stage.

Did you see the two characters progressing at the same speed?

AMM: Lyra's very open, she embraces people straight off. She's very earnest in the way she collects people along the way, she's very open to love people like Roger and Iorek, whereas Will is a very guarded and troubled child.

DC: They progress in the way they learn from each other, and how they deal with people.

Do you have to agree with each other about what both your characters are thinking?

AMM: I think you do. I know what Dominic's thinking about as Will, those things just grow. But there's always a point in rehearsal where you think "Oh, I haven't got any kind of grip on this character" and you just panic. I think that was the point when we sat down and talked about it. Then when you've done that it's fine, you can get on and play it.

DC: There was an amazing book we had in rehearsal, which we called "The Bible". Someone had gone through all the books and written down a description of every character, of how characters describe one another or how they feel about one another, with the page references. So you could always refer back to that.

When you started performing in front of an audience, did that give you another sense of your character?

AMM: Yes, it was brilliant, wasn't it? We always talk about how our Cittàgazze scene was dead as a dodo in the rehearsal room, but when we got in front of an audience it completely changed.

DC: Will is a character that people know is going to come on, they've been waiting for that moment.

AMM: We'd grown used to how different Will and Lyra are, but then you get an audience laughing at the fact that this boy doesn't know anything about daemons.

And Will is like the audience, in a way, isn't he, because he's having to learn about Lyra's world in the same way the audience did.

DC: It's nice because the audience is ahead of him. Will becomes the ridiculous one because he thinks Pantalaimon is a pet, a talking cat. They're ahead of the game.

What's it like, Anna, acting with someone else playing part of your character—Samuel Barnett plays your daemon Pantalaimon. Did you have to agree with him what your character was like?

AMM: Yes, we did. Pan has a very distinctive character of his own. So we did discuss a lot, not only in terms of choreography. It was quite frustrating, we spent a week with Aletta Collins, trying to work out where I would be, where Sam would be. Usually in a play you can just walk around freely, but we had to find a way of moving together, so I didn't fall over him. Eventually we found a way of listening to each other and knowing where the other was. The characters are *so* distinctive in the books, though, that I think we found it quite easy to establish what was Lyra and what was Pan.

All three of you—Sam, Anna and Dominic—were at drama school together. Did that help you? Did you learn to prepare a character in the same way?

AMM: I was scared of Dom at drama school; he was far too cool for me!

DC: I suppose it helped in the sense that we'd all had the same training.

AMM: Sam and I were in the same year, and were very dear friends as well. So I'd just go "Sam, stand there!"

Do you use the training you had at drama school in preparing a character?

DC: Yes, you obviously get rid of a lot of it, but coming to a theatre like this, I can't imagine not having that experience of learning the very basic things.

What did you learn about playing twelve-year-olds?

DC: We were quite keen not to do 'child acting' in terms of squeaky voices and scratching bums. And I think Nick Hytner was quite keen not to have that.

AMM: The hardest thing about child acting is the energy you have to have to play a child. When you're in your mid-twenties, that's quite hard.

And you have to be very direct in your thoughts.

AMM: Yes, you can't think too much. In a way, it's quite liberating. I found it very hard, but Nick was there saying "Just do it, just get on with it."

DC: And the writing, too, has an energy to it.

AMM: I found it hard to understand how Lyra could flip from one thing to another, but actually children do. It's only as adults that you start to over-analyse, but children get on with life, accept things.

DC: Some of their decisions, the things they do—I don't think any grown-up would cut a window and jump through to another world—it's instinctive.

How has your performance changed through the run?

AMM: Dominic's performance has become increasingly naughty, making it *very* difficult for me to work...

DC: I suppose you have to try to make it real and fresh each time. We do a lot of performances, eight shows a week; when you do that you're thinking on the line much more, other things come into your head about how to approach a scene.

AMM: That's the nice thing about it, you sometimes have a really big revelation about something that hadn't occurred to you before, and you can change it.

What are you looking for in the person you are acting with?

AMM: It's very frustrating if you're working with someone who can't communicate with you, or they're in their own mindset. As long as you can communicate...

DC: That was something we learnt at drama school—listening to someone on stage, and looking into their eyes.

Does your relationship change from performance to performance?

AMM: Yes, not dramatically. We already had quite a good rapport, so we don't feel the need to push that.

What advice did Philip Pullman give you about your characters or performances?

DC: He's been wonderful throughout, only ever said things that would help the stories progress and has left the other side completely to Nick.

AMM: The scariest thing for us was when Philip came into rehearsals because you want so much to get it right, to bring someone to life who has come from his imagination. It would be awful to get it horribly wrong.

Audience questions

Could you tell us why Mary Malone wasn't in the play?

AMM: She was a huge part of the books, but in the adaptation a lot of things had to be sacrificed, and that was a big chunk of it. When Philip Pullman read the books on tape, I think it took 36 hours, and we only had six hours for the play. So Mary Malone was one of the things that had to go.

Which was your favourite shape your daemon Pan took?

AMM: I'm not sure. I'm very attached to both the wildcat and the pine marten and I flip between the two of them. I think *probably* the pine marten...

What's your feeling at the end of this run, knowing you may come back to it?

DC: It's been such a huge project and it's been going on so long, over a year and a half since we started the workshops. It's nice to think that perhaps it will change next year and we will be part of it again. It's always rather sad to leave something.

Could you give some advice to children wanting to get involved in acting?

DC: Join youth theatres, get involved at school, do evening classes, try to get into a drama school at some stage... I started at primary school.

AMM: When I was twelve I started taking acting classes and got involved that way.

Who do you think Lyra preferred, her mother or her father?

AMM: That's such a good question. I think 'prefer' is probably the wrong word. I think she wanted them both to want her and love her but as a young girl there's always a bond with your daddy, and I think she wanted this man to be her ideal father, so I think maybe she would have preferred a stronger bond with him, or for him to display more love and affection towards her.

How different is it performing the two shows on the same day, as opposed to doing one on one day and the other on the next?

DC: I think it's really good to do them both in sequence, knowing a lot of the audience has been with you throughout that journey. I've always really enjoyed doing both together.

AMM: Me too.

DC: You sometimes feel at the end of the first one that you haven't really finished it, and some people aren't able to come back and see the second one. But when you've been there throughout the day it's like an event, and at the end of a double day, the crew all come out and take a bow too, and it feels as if you've all been on a long journey together.

What's your favourite part of the play?

AMM: Mine is when I get to Cittàgazze and meet Will. I love that scene; it's quite long so there's lots of room to play around. When Lyra meets Will, that's it. She's always had Pan with her, but he's part of her. When she finds Will that's it, and they go on a journey together. As an actor I feel the burden is shared after that; Sam and I breathe a sigh of relief.

DC: I've always felt the same about that scene, but I also love doing the end. I find it very hard and sad but I do love doing it, discovering his daemon and having to say good-bye to Lyra, but knowing they're doing it for all the right reasons—and I'll see her again next day, so it's all OK.

Was coming off the script a very gradual process?

AMM: No, it was really quick. I never really had to sit down and learn it. We had twelve weeks rehearsal and it went in really quickly. It's not like learning Shakespeare, it's quite simple to learn and it just seemed to go in.

Were you given new scenes to learn during rehearsal?

DC: Yes, but we did seem to pick them up straight away.

Do you have any feelings about this production coming to the States?

DC: We desperately want it to go to the States, but apparently it doesn't fit into any other theatre in the world.

AMM: There were talks about it going to Broadway, and we were planning our shopping, but apparently the Olivier is the only theatre that has this drum revolve, so it's not possible to do this production anywhere else.

What's it like acting with such complex scenery?

AMM: Like having a nervous breakdown!

DC: On the first day of rehearsal we were shown what was going to happen, but I don't think any of us understood that this huge round thing was going to come up out of the floor, spin you round and drop you out the other side. The delay in our first preview was for technical reasons, and you are, for the first few days or weeks a bit worried about what might come and chop your head off.

AMM: This drum goes right down to the bottom of the theatre and sometimes you get taken right down to the bottom, spat out, then have to run up here to the third floor and carry on. I found it a nightmare technically, that was the only negative thing about it. I found it really scary. Some moments felt hairy at the time, it's a big space and there are loud noises, and it's a different discipline; you're on a stage that's moving all the time. I'm mostly in plays where there are three people in a room, a few chairs, and you talk to one another. This is a very different concept and I wish I could watch the whole show, I have no idea what it looks like.

Are there any plans for it to be filmed here in situ?

DC: No, I don't think so. But I think there is always a library record video, and we have been filming various scenes for the new educational website [stagework.org].

How did you prepare for the scene where the two characters fall in love with each other?

AMM: Actually I found it quite nerve-wracking, the scene when Lyra says "I love you" and shoves a load of raspberries in his mouth. It's such an intimate moment, a wonderfully beautiful intimate moment. I felt childlike, that nervous thing Lyra must have felt. Those scenes are always quite difficult to get into at first as an actor. Then you get used to them and it's fine.

DC: Nick made us very comfortable, we did it for the first time in a smaller rehearsal room, and we laughed our way through it.

I've read that Philip Pullman's favourite part of writing the book was when Will meets Iorek. Did he give you any guidance?

DC: He didn't personally give me any guidance but I know he had a lot to do with changing the scene for the stage. In the book they're in the water and there are a lot of flame-throwers going on, and I think Philip wanted that moment to be spectacular and terrifying. I think that's one particular point that next year will be changed.

How did it feel knowing that almost everyone coming to the play has a vision of what your character should be?

AMM: I'm having therapy at the moment…That was the thing that preyed on my mind quite a lot before I even accepted the job because these books had been so special to me, close to my heart, before I knew about the plays. You build the world in your own head, and of course Lyra is an incredible character and I've been so fortunate to be able to play her. So it did plague me quite a lot, that pressure that people have their own idea of her. Then I just thought, Hey, people are going to be disappointed. If I'm lucky, half the people who come here will like what I've done with it, and half will think "That's not how I saw her". There's nothing I can do about that. All I can do is be as true as I can to what I thought she was from what Philip has written and how Nicholas has adapted it, that's all I can do.

If you each had a daemon sitting beside you on stage now, what daemon would you choose?

DC: I think it would be a cat, I don't know why.

AMM: It's funny because I was talking to some friends about this last night, and all of them were saying they thought I'd have some sort of monkey, or a baby form of an animal—incredibly immature!

Do you feel the reaction to the play has increased in enthusiasm during the run?

DC: Yes, perhaps because some people have waited so long to see the end of the story.

AMM: It keeps you on your toes, keeps you mindful of the fact that people expect a lot from this show, they have high expectations. So you don't sit back.

Do you think it's improved during the run?

AMM: Yes, it's definitely improved. Now it's a very smooth-running machine. Shows always are complicated to begin with but now everyone can do it with their eyes shut, so of course it's a better show.

It seemed to generate a tremendous energy between the actors and the audience.

AMM: That's wonderful to hear because this is such a huge auditorium that we don't always know how people in the audience feel.

www.ingramcontent.com/pod-product-compliance
Ingram Content Group UK Ltd.
Pitfield, Milton Keynes, MK11 3LW, UK
UKHW020706280225
455688UK00012B/286